*Understanding*
*Macroeconomics*

*Other books by Robert L. Heilbroner*

THE WORLDLY PHILOSOPHERS

THE QUEST FOR WEALTH

THE FUTURE AS HISTORY

THE MAKING OF ECONOMIC SOCIETY

THE GREAT ASCENT

A PRIMER ON GOVERNMENT SPENDING *(with Peter L. Bernstein)*

Robert L. Heilbroner

# Under-standing Macro-economics

PRENTICE-HALL, INC. ENGLEWOOD CLIFFS, N.J.

Current printing (last digit):

13  12  11  10  9  8  7  6  5  4

*Library of Congress Catalog Card No. 65–16577*

*Printed in the United States of America*
C-93594

PRENTICE-HALL INTERNATIONAL, INC., *London*
PRENTICE-HALL OF AUSTRALIA, PTY., LTD., *Sydney*
PRENTICE-HALL OF CANADA, LTD., *Toronto*
PRENTICE-HALL OF INDIA (PRIVATE) LTD., *New Delhi*
PRENTICE-HALL OF JAPAN, INC., *Tokyo*

For
*Hans Neisser*

# *Preface*

The purpose of this book is to present the main themes of macroeconomics as simply and lucidly as possible, not only so that its readers can pass their exams, but in the more ambitious hope that long after these exams have faded into oblivion, something of the central ideas and conclusions of contemporary economics will remain.

The problem in a book of this kind is not just how to present the material, but where to draw the line—a matter that cannot, I fear, be resolved to everyone's satisfaction. The instructor who has spent years acquiring a knowledge of the subleties and complexities of economic relationships is sure to feel that too much has been left out. The student who has a semester or two to absorb all the formal economic instruction he is likely to receive in his life is apt to feel just the opposite. By way of apology to both, I can say only that I have thought hard about where I *have* drawn the line, emphasizing and highlighting certain basic processes of great conceptual and practical importance and minimizing side issues of secondary interest. Whether I will now succeed either in helping my readers over their exams or in giving them an understanding of economics that will "stick" are questions to which I shall be just as eager as they are to learn the answers.

A number of people have helped me very greatly in this book, and I should like to thank them for their pains. Hans Neisser of the Graduate Faculty of the New School for Social Research strengthened the manuscript substantially with his critical comments. In gratitude for this and previous assistance, and in partial payment of a long-standing debt of student to teacher and of colleague to friend, I am happy to dedicate this book to him. I am deeply indebted also to another New School colleague and devoted friend, Peter L. Bernstein, who read the manuscript twice with meticulous care. There is not a page that has not benefited from his searching criticism and good advice. Harry G. Johnson of the University of Chicago gave me generously of his time and provided an invaluable critique. Eli Ginzberg of Columbia University pointed out several weak points in the text and was especially helpful in regard to the chapter on employment, and Carey Thompson of the University of Texas performed a similarly useful task, with particular emphasis on the chapter on money. Finally, I am happy to acknowledge the counsel of Adolph Lowe, now Professor Emeritus at my teaching institution. Quite aside from his discerning comments, this book, like all my previous ones, is an expression of an interest in, and orientation toward, economics that I received in large measure from him. It remains only to add the usual proviso, absolving all the above from the errors of omission and commission from which even their combined thoughtful efforts could not save me.

*New York and Chilmark*

ROBERT L. HEILBRONER

# Contents

# 4

# Saving and Investment 43

# 5

# The Consumption Sector 60

# 6

# The Investment Sector 77

# 1

# *Introduction*

Powerful forces range over the American economy today. Technological advances of startling impact, swift changes in population, new climates of affluence, newly rediscovered realities of poverty—all have become part of our accustomed headline fare, part of the background of our daily lives. Perhaps more noticeable than any of these is a phenomenon still remembered by the generation of the middle-aged, but ignored until a few years ago by the generation of the young—a sucking undertow of unemployment. For the last half-decade the problem of finding a job—or worse, of not finding a job—has been the major worry of over four million Americans. Thus it is hardly surprising that the condition of, and the prospects for, the American economy have become subjects for concerned discussion and debate, not only in political life but in the home and on the campus.

At the center of the discussion is a recently minted but already familiar word: automation. Anyone who has gone into a modern factory and has seen the extraordinarily sensitive, dexterous, and powerful equipment by which production is now facilitated must have asked himself what effect these new machines—

so much quicker, stronger, more accurate, and cheaper than men
—would have on the capacity of ordinary people to earn their
livelihoods. Anyone who has gone into a modern office and has
seen tasks that were once the jealous prerogatives of skilled clerks
and junior managers now performed by silent banks of computers and clunking batteries of electric printers must have had
the same thought brought home even more disturbingly. Certainly automation, as the contemporary manifestation of the
long technological revolution, poses threats to the traditional
working of the economy that cannot be lightly shrugged aside.

But automation is not the only economic challenge of our
times. The growth of our population—or rather, the peculiar
contemporary pattern of that growth—poses another. What was
once a bumper crop of war babies has now burst through our
school system and is about to emerge, en masse, onto the market
for jobs. Even if these young workers were not confronted with
a new technological environment, the problem of digesting them
would not be easy. Between 1950 and 1960 the labor force aged
fourteen to twenty-four increased by less than 600,000; between
1960 and 1970 this group will increase by more than six *million*.
Never before has it been necessary to find jobs for so many new
workers in so short a space of time, and already we are experi-
encing difficulties in doing so. In 1963, one out of every seven
teenagers in search of work found none. Among nonwhite teenagers, the rate of failure was almost one in three. And the full
brunt of the wave of young job-seekers is still to come.

Meanwhile we have come to speak of affluence and poverty
in rapid succession. The 1950's gave us the first breathtaking—
although not entirely agreeable—vision of an affluent society.
Shortly thereafter the rising unemployment of the 1960's suddenly called to our attention that we were still a society in which
wealth and poverty can and do exist side by side. One quarter of
all our nonfarm families now make more than $10,000 a year.
Yet—depending on whether one defines poverty as subsistence,
adequacy, or minimum comfort—twenty, forty, or seventy million
people in the United States are still poor. And whereas a comparison with the statistics of past poverty offers some reassurance

on this score (although not quite so much as we often assume), it is small consolation for those who find themselves in one or another of the disprivileged categories to be told that there are fewer like themselves than there were thirty or sixty years ago.

These are some of the uncomfortable actualities about which this book is written. Employment and unemployment, men and machines, affluence and poverty are the central objects of its concern, the central problems with which it will deal. Yet it is well that we emphasize at the outset that our purpose is not merely economic description. Someone who wants a close account of what it is like to be unemployed or poor, or of how particular machines can be used to displace labor, must consult another book. Here we are embarked on a generalized study of the *relationships* and *processes* that underlie these problems, not in a detailed examination of the problems themselves as they manifest themselves in "real life."

For many who first enter the study of economics, this emphasis on abstract relationships rather than on the concrete details of life comes as a disappointment. It seems to turn economics away from the genuine moral content of social issues and to divorce it from that which is most interesting and important in economic life. But there is a reason for this generalizing emphasis of economic thought. It is that we cannot understand—indeed, we cannot even clearly visualize—what is wrong with the economic world until we have come to comprehend in the first place how that world works.

Hence this book is directed first of all at giving us a picture of economic society as a working mechanism, a vast, intricate—and yet comprehensible—social machine for provisioning a human community. What we will try to learn about that mechanism is not the facts and figures of a particular economic situation or of a particular year's problems, but the meshing of basic processes and the structure of lasting relationships. Then it will be time to turn to more immediate issues. Once we have acquired a systematic grasp of the way our economy is constructed, it will not be difficult to fit the newspaper headlines into our over-all knowledge, nor to infuse our intelligence with feeling.

Yet to learn something of the grand mechanics of a society requires a special effort, perhaps even a touch of a special gift. It is seemingly a very small effort, a very minor gift, but on it hinges more than anything else the ability to understand how the economic system operates. That effort is the willingness to abandon our familiar vantage point on economic life for a new and sometimes disconcerting one. It is our capacity to leave behind an acquaintance with the economic scene as individual participants, and to enter upon a new view from which we can see all our economic activities at once, simultaneously and collectively—a view that embraces not the actions of a single person or firm or town, but that looks out over an entire society. Of all the intellectual demands made by economics, this first leap to the economist's perch is perhaps the most difficult. But it is also the most necessary, for only after we have gained this lofty vantage point can we begin to see the extraordinary panorama with which economics deals.

# 2

# *Wealth and Output*

What does an economy look like from the Olympian perspective of the economist?

The spectacle is not unlike that from a plane. What we see first is the fundamental tableau of nature—the fields and forests, lakes and seas, with their inherent riches; then the diverse artifacts of man—the cities and towns, the road and rail networks, the factories and machines, the stocks of half-completed or unsold goods; and finally the human actors themselves with all their skills and talents, their energies, their social organization.

Thus our perspective shows us a vast panorama from which we single out for our special attention those elements and activities having to do with our worldly well-being, with our capacity to provide ourselves with the necessaries and luxuries of material life. It need hardly be said that this is at best only a partial view of society. An economist does not examine the flux of social goings-on, the quality of intellectual life, the spirituality or crassness of a community. Initially, at any rate, he concerns himself with only those aspects of society that bear on its *material provisioning,* and even here he often limits himself to things that he can measure in some fairly objective way.

## The National Wealth

Let us, then, begin to set our first economic impressions in order by directing our attention to an attribute of the landscape below us that is clearly important in the provisioning process, and that should be subject to roughly accurate measurement— our national wealth. By our wealth, we mean the very objects

Table 2-1   UNITED STATES NATIONAL WEALTH: 1958 VALUE*

|  | Billions of dollars |
|---|---|
| **Buildings and structures** | |
| Residential housing other than farm | 392 |
| Business, institutional and farm buildings | 273 |
| Government structures | 168 |
| **Equipment** | |
| Producers' equipment (machines, factories, etc.) | 200 |
| Consumer durable goods, such as autos, and major appliances | 179 |
| **Inventories** | |
| Livestock | 18 |
| Crop | 8 |
| Business | 96 |
| Public | 8 |
| **Monetary gold and silver** | 25 |
| **Land** | |
| Farm | 88 |
| Forests | 14 |
| Nonfarm | 149 |
| Public | 41 |
| **Net foreign assets** | 24 |
| TOTAL | 1,683 |

* Rather than encumber each table with sources that are, for the most part, identical, I have added the source only if the figures might be difficult to find or if they are the result of considerable arithmetical manipulation. All unidentified figures will be found in one or more of the following three basic sourcebooks: *Historical Statistics of the United States, 1960*, and *Statistical Abstract of the United States, 1963*, both published in Washington, D.C., by the Bureau of the Census; and *Survey of Current Business* (July 1964), a publication of the Office of Business Economics, Department of Commerce, Washington, D.C.

—or at least many of them—that have already caught our eye. The table on the preceding page is the last estimate made of the national wealth of the United States for the year 1958.

Let us note immediately that this is not a full valuation of the riches of our society. No monetary worth is put on our human skills or even on the presence of so many heads of population. Nor does this table pretend to embrace, much less measure, all our material possessions. Such immense economic treasures as the contents of the Library of Congress or the Patent Office cannot be accurately valued. Nor can works of art, nor military equipment—neither of which is included in the total. Much of our public lands are valued at no more than nominal amounts. Hence at best this is the roughest of estimates. Nonetheless, it gives us an idea of the magnitude of the economic endowment that we have at our disposal.

It would perhaps be a much more meaningful idea if we could now compare our own national wealth with that of a poor nation, such as India, or more precisely, compare the *per capita* value of our wealth—that is, the share of our wealth that is available to each of us—to the *per capita* wealth of India. Alas, as is so often the case with the less developed countries, such statistics do not exist for India. But perhaps we can get a glimmering of what such a comparison might show by comparing a few items for which we do have figures.

Table 2-2    COMPARATIVE WEALTH STATISTICS, INDIA AND U.S., RECENT YEARS*

|  | United States | India |
|---|---|---|
|  | Per 1,000 People | |
| Motor vehicles in use | 422 | 1 |
| Telephones | 430 | 1 |
| Radios | 944 | 5 |

* Years vary; see source: *Statistical Abstract*, 1963, pp. 930, 932.

It is clear enough that if we could total up all the items in both nations, the scales would tilt overwhelmingly in favor of the United States. That this has an immense significance for the relative well-being of the two countries is apparent. However, let us defer a consideration of exactly what that significance is, until we look a little more closely into the nature of national wealth itself.

## Capital

One portion of the endowment of a nation's wealth has a special significance. This is its national *capital*—the portion of its productive wealth that is *man-made* and therefore *reproducible*. If we look back at the table, we can see that our own national capital in 1958 consisted of the sum total of all our structures, our producers' equipment and our consumer durables, our inventories, our monetary gold and silver, and our foreign assets—$1,391 billions in all.

We can think of this national capital as consisting of whatever has been preserved out of the sum total of everything that has ever been produced from the very beginning of the economic history of the United States up to a certain date—here December 31, 1958. Needless to say, some of that capital—inventories for example—might be used up the very next day. On the other hand, inventories might also be increased. In fact, our national capital changes from date to date, as we do add to our inventories, or to our stocks of equipment or structures, etc.—or, more rarely, as we consume them and do not replace them. But at any date, our capital still represents *all that the nation has produced* —yesterday or a century ago—*and that it has not used up or destroyed.*

The reason that we identify our national capital within the larger frame of our wealth is that it is constantly changing and usually growing. Not that a nation's inheritance of natural resources is unimportant; indeed, the ability of a people to build capital depends to no small degree on the bounties or obstacles offered by its geography and geology—witness the economic limitations imposed by desert and ice on the Bedouin and the Eskimo. But the point in singling out our capital is that it represents the portion of our total national endowment over which we have the most immediate control. As we shall later see, much of a nation's current economic fortunes is intimately related to the rate at which it is adding to its capital wealth.

## Wealth and Claims

There remains to be noted one more thing before we leave the subject of wealth. In our table of national wealth, two items are missing that would be the very first to be counted in an inventory of our personal wealth: our bank accounts and our financial assets, such as stocks or bonds or deeds or mortgages. Why are these all-important items of personal wealth excluded from our summary of national wealth?

The answer to this seeming paradox is not hard to find. We have already counted the *things*—the houses, factories, machines, etc.,—that constitute the real assets behind stocks, bonds, deeds, and the like. Indeed these certificates tell us only who *owns* the various items of our national capital. Stocks and bonds and mortgages and deeds are *claims* on assets, but they are not those assets in themselves. The reality of General Motors is its physical plant and its going organization, not the shares of stock that organization has issued. If by some curious mischance all its shares disintegrated, General Motors would still be there; but if the plants and the organization disintegrated instead, the shares would not magically constitute for us another enterprise.

So, too, with our bank accounts. The dollars we spend or hold in our accounts are part of our personal wealth only insofar as they command goods or services. The value of coin or currency as "objects" is much less than their official and legal value as money. But most of the goods over which our money exerts its claims (although not, it must be admitted, the services it also buys) are already on our balance sheet. To count our money as part of national wealth would thus be to count a claim as if it were an asset, much as in the case of stocks and bonds.

Why, then, do we have an item for monetary gold and silver (mainly gold) in our table of national wealth? The answer is that under existing international arrangements, foreigners will accept gold in exchange for their own real assets (whereas they are not bound to accept our dollar bills), and that, therefore, monetary gold gives us a claim against *foreign* wealth. In much the same way, the item of *net foreign assets* represents the value of real assets located in other nations but owned by U.S. citizens, less the value of any real wealth located in the United States and owned by foreigners.

Thus we reach a very important final conclusion. National wealth is not quite the same thing as the sum of personal wealth. When we add up our individual wealth, we include first of all our holdings of money or stocks or bonds—all items that are excluded from our national register of wealth. The difference is that as individuals, we properly consider our own wealth to be the *claims* we have against one another, whereas, as a society, we consider our wealth to be the stock of material *assets* we possess, and the only claims we consider are those that we may have against other societies. National wealth is a *real* phenomenon, the tangible consequence of past production. Financial wealth, on the other hand—the form in which individuals hold their wealth —is only the way the claims of ownership are established vis-à-vis the underlying real assets of the community. The contrast between the underlying, slow-changing reality of national wealth and the overlying, sometimes fast-changing financial representation of that wealth is one of the differences between economic life viewed from the vantage point of the economist and that same life seen through the eyes of a participant in the process. We shall encounter many more such contrasts as our study proceeds.

## Wealth and Output

But why is national wealth so important? Exactly what is the connection between the wealth of nations and the well-being of their citizens?

The question is not an idle one, for the connection between wealth and well-being is not a matter of direct physical cause and effect. After all, India has the largest inventory of livestock in the world, but its contribution to Indian living standards is far less than that of our livestock wealth. Or again, our national capital in 1933 was not significantly different from that in 1929, but one year was marked by widespread misery and the other by booming prosperity. Clearly then, the existence of great physical wealth by itself does not guarantee—it only holds out the possibility of—a high standard of living. It is only insofar as wealth interacts with the working population that it exerts its enormous economic leverage, and this interaction is not a mechanical phenomenon that we can take for granted, but a complex *social* process, whose motivations we most explore.

As the example of Indian livestock indicates, local customs and beliefs can effectively sterilize the potential physical benefits of wealth. Perhaps we should generalize that conclusion by observing that the political and social system will have a primary role in causing an effective or ineffective use of existing wealth. Compare the traditional hoarding of gold or gems in many backward societies with the possibility of their disposal to procure foreign exchange for the purchase of machinery.

In a modern industrial society, we take for granted some kind of effective social and political structure. Then why do we at times make vigorous use of our existing material assets and at other times seem to put them to little or no use? Why do we have "good times" and "bad times"? The question directs our attention back to the panorama of society to discover something further about its economic operation.

### The Factors of Production

This time, our gaze fastens on a different aspect of the tableau. Rather than noticing our stock of wealth, we note the result of our use of that wealth, a result we can see emerging in the form of a *flow of production*.

How does this flow of production arise? We can see that it comes into being as man combines his energies with his natural and man-made environment. To assist us in understanding this crucial process, we classify the cooperating elements in the production process into three categories.

Into the first of these we put the resources of nature itself—

the land and waters and their riches—and to this essential element in production we give the name Land. Into a second category we place those man-made artifacts that are of such vital importance in nearly every economic activity. To these we give the name Capital. And finally, to human activity in the economic process, however simple or complicated, we give the title Labor. These three categories, Land, Capital, and Labor, we call the *factors of production*. It is a useful term, for it enables us to sum up in a phrase the component agencies needed to bring about production.

## *The Social Meaning of the Factors of Production*

We will be speaking of the factors of production throughout this book, but we should not leave them in this introduction without making clear one further point. When we speak of combining land, labor, and capital, we are really talking about two related, and yet distinct, things. Partly we refer to the *physical* combination of the soil or its wealth, of machines, buildings, etc., and of human effort. This engineering aspect of production is, needless to say, of great importance. But when we talk about "the factors of production," we do not mean only this technical side of things. We mean also that different *social* functions have to be combined in various ways, if the production process is to be carried out.

For in our society, land, labor, and capital are all privately owned. This is not true in every society. In some tribal societies, for instance, land is communally owned and not available for purchase or rent from a single owner. In many societies in history, labor has been performed by serfs or slaves who did not "own" their labor in the sense of being able to offer it as free agents for a price. Today, in the communist countries, capital and land are both usually owned by the state, and not by a private person. Only in our kind of economic society—capitalism—are the great bulk of the physical agencies of production privately owned.

Hence when we speak of combining the factors of production, we are speaking not only of a process of engineering, but also of a *social process*—a system of rewards and penalties, sanctions and inducements that motivates the owners of the physical agencies to offer their services for use in the production process.

## Micro- and Macroeconomics

Much of economics is an attempt to analyze how a society of privately owned land, labor, and capital (each possessing its particular physical attributes) will in fact be combined into production.

When economics focuses its study on the individual agents of the process, the individual owner of labor or capital or land, or when it highlights the manner in which a typical entrepreneur organizes land, labor, and capital in his firm, we call the resulting study *microeconomics*. When, however, economics opens its lens to the widest possible extent, to study not so much the individual participant in the production process but the total activity of all participants, we call the study *macroeconomics*.

We will not venture into the world of microeconomics, the world of the individual entrepreneur or the individual consumer or worker, but we must understand something of the background against which both the micro- and the macroeconomic processes work. This is the presence of an *all-embracing market* on which the factors can offer their services—the landowner offering the use of his land; the capitalist, the use of his capital; the worker, the use of his labor—a market on which, as well, the entrepreneur can bid for these services. On this vast market, not only are the *services* of the factors bought and sold, as entrepreneurs hire labor, rent land, and borrow capital; but the *products* created by these employed factors are also sold here by the entrepreneurs.

This ubiquitous market network, where both factors of production, and goods and services are bought and sold, is an essential feature of our economic system. Like private property, however, it should not be too easily taken for granted. Many economies do not have a highly developed market network. Traditional societies in the underdeveloped world, for instance, often have no real market for labor, so that village laborers do not earn *wages* determined by the supply of, and demand for, their labor, but are paid a sum determined by long-standing custom or by some powerful personage. In the same way, some societies do not have a market for land—feudalism, for instance, did not—so that landlords do not earn a rent determined by the supply and demand for land, but simply expropriate a traditional share of the crops grown on their holdings. Or again, markets for capital may not exist (as in the U.S.S.R.), so that no one will earn interest or profit for making his capital available to an entrepreneur.

Our introduction to the factors of production has thus given us insight into much more than just the possibility of classifying the variety of economic activity into the simple categories of land, labor, and capital. In turn, these categories have told us something of the historic evolution of our society and have alerted us to its all-important institutions of private property and the market.

## The Flow of Production

We have lingered long enough over the factors. Now let us move on to watch the process for whose clarification we originally stopped to classify the factors themselves.

We have learned, in our new vocabulary, that production takes place by the combination of the services of the factors of production organized through the marketplace. Now what happens to that flow of production as it leaves the hands of the entrepreneurs who brought it into existence?

It may help us picture the flow as a whole if we imagine that each and every good and service that is produced—each loaf of bread, each nut and bolt, each doctor's call, each theatrical performance, each car, ship, lathe, or bolt of cloth—can be identified in the way that a radioactive isotope allows us to follow the circulation of certain kinds of cells through the body. Then if we look down on the economic panorama, we can see the continuous combination of land, labor, and capital giving off a continuous flow of "light," as goods and services emerge in their saleable form.

Where do these lights go? Many, as we can see, are soon extinguished. The goods or services they represent have been incorporated into other products to form more fully finished items of output. Thus from our aerial perspective we can follow a finished product, such as cotton, from the fields to the spinning mill, where its light is extinguished, for there the cotton disappears into a new "finished" product, yarn. In turn, the light of the yarn traces a path as it leaves the spinning mill by way of sale to the textile mill, there to be doused as the yarn disappears into a new finished good, cloth. And again, the cloth leaving the textile mill lights a way to the factory where it will become part of an article of clothing.

## The Consumption Flow

And what of the clothing? Here at last we have what the economist calls a *final* good. Why "final"? Because once in the possession of its ultimate owner, the clothing passes out of the active economic flow. As a good in the hands of a consumer, it is no longer an object on the marketplace. Its light is now extinguished permanently—or if we wish to complete our image, we can imagine it fading gradually as the clothing "disappears" into the use and pleasure, the so-called "utility," of the consumer. In the case of consumer goods like food, or of consumer services like recreation, the light goes out faster, for these items are literally "consumed" when they reach their final destination.

We shall have a good deal to learn in later chapters about the behavior of consumers. What we should notice in this first macroeconomic view is the supreme importance of this flow of production into consumers' hands. This is the vital process by which the population replenishes or increases its energies and ministers to its wants and needs; it is a process that, if halted for very long, would cause a society to perish. That is why we speak of consumption as the ultimate end and aim of all economic activity.

## The Investment Flow

For all the importance of consumption, if we look down on the illuminated flow of output we see a surprising thing. Whereas the greater portion of the final goods and services of the economy is bought by the human agents of production for their consumption, we also find that a lesser but still considerable flow of final products is not. What happens to it?

If we follow an appropriate good, we may find out. Let us watch the destination of the steel that leaves a Pittsburgh mill. Some of it, like our cotton cloth, will become incorporated into consumers' goods, ending up as "tin" cans, automobiles, or household articles of various kinds. But some steel will not find its way to a consumer at all; instead, it will end up as part of a machine or an office building or a railroad track.

Now in a way, these goods are not "final," for they are used to produce still further goods or services—the machine producing output of some kind, the building producing office space, the rail track producing transportation. Yet there is a difference between such goods, used for production, and consumer goods, like clothing. The difference is that the machine, the office building, and the track are not goods that are simply used up, or "consumed," as they give off their useful functions. Instead, they are usually carefully maintained and replaced when they wear out. In terms of our image, these goods do not lose their light as they reach their final destination, but there they continue to burn. That is why we call them *capital goods* in distinction to consumers' goods. As part of our capital, they will be preserved, maintained, and renewed, perhaps indefinitely. Hence *the stock of capital, like consumers, constitutes a final destination for output.**

## Gross and Net Investment

We call the great stream of output that goes to capital *gross investment*. The very word *gross* suggests that it conceals a finer breakdown; and looking more closely, we can see that the flow of output going to capital does indeed serve two distinct purposes. Part of it is used to replace the capital—the machines, the build-

---

* We might note that some products, like automobiles, possess characteristics of both consumption goods and capital goods. We call such goods *consumer durables;* and unlike ordinary goods (such as clothing) held by consumers, we include them in our inventory of national wealth (see Table 2-1, p. 6).

ings, the track, or whatever—that has been used up in the process of production. Just as the human agents of production have to be replenished by a flow of consumption goods, so the material agents of production need to be maintained and renewed if their contribution to output is to remain undiminished. We call the part of gross investment, whose purpose is to keep society's stock of capital intact, *replacement investment,* or simply *replacement.*

Sometimes the total flow of output going to capital is not large enough to maintain the existing stock—for instance, if we allow inventories (a form of capital) to become depleted, or if we simply fail to replace worn-out equipment or plant. We call this running-down of capital *disinvestment,* meaning by the phrase the very opposite of investment: instead of building up capital, we are literally consuming it.

Not all gross investment is used for replacement purposes, however. Some of the flow may *increase* the stock of capital, adding machines, buildings, track, etc. If the total output consigned to capital is sufficiently great not only to make up for wear and tear, but to increase the capital stock, we say there has been *new* or *net investment,* or *net capital formation.*

One last important point. Who normally buys these additions to our capital wealth? In the main, the purchasers are business firms who seek to increase their holdings of machines and buildings and equipment of various kinds. Since additions to business capital are additions to our nation's wealth, and since with more wealth we would expect to be able to produce still more goods and services, the act of business investment immediately stands out as a key element in the study of macroeconomics. In fact, as we shall see, in many ways the process and the problems of business investment will be a central point of focus in our book.

### Consumption and Investment

A simple diagram may help us picture the flows of output we have been discussing.

The diagram calls to our attention three important attributes of the economic system.

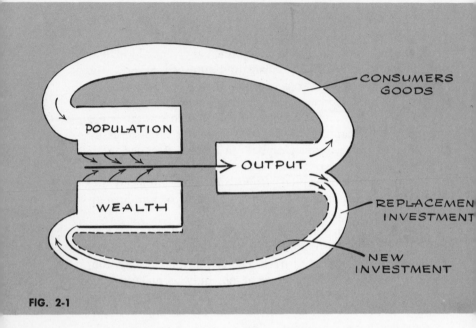

**FIG. 2-1**

1. It emphasizes the essential circularity, the self-renewing, self-feeding nature of the production flow. This circularity is a feature of the macroeconomic process to which we will return again and again.

2. It illumines a basic choice that all economic societies must make: *a choice between consumption and investment.* For the split flow of production reveals that every good entering the capital stream cannot also be in the consumption stream. At any given level of output, consumption and investment are, so to speak, rivals for the current output of society.

3. Finally, it makes clear that *society can invest* (that is, add to its capital) *only the output that it refrains from consuming.* We call this relinquishing of consumption *saving,* and saving thus becomes an economic act located at the very core of the wealth-creation process. For the economic meaning of saving, as our diagram shows, is to release resources from consumption so

that they can be used for the building of capital. Whether they *will* be so used is a matter that will occupy us through many subsequent chapters.

## Gross National Product

There remains but one preliminary matter before we proceed to a closer examination of the actual determinants of the flow of production. We have seen that the annual output of the nation is a revealing measure of its well-being, for it reflects the degree of interaction between the population and its wealth. Later we shall also find output to be a major determinant of employment. Hence it behooves us to examine the nature and general character of this flow and to become familiar with its nomenclature and composition.

We call the dollar value of the total annual output of final goods in the nation its *gross national product*. The gross national product (or GNP as it is usually abbreviated) is thus nothing but the dollar value of the total output of all consumption goods and of all investment goods including increases in inventories. As such we are already familiar with its general meaning. At this juncture, however, we must define GNP a little more precisely.

1. *GNP includes only final goods.* We are interested, through the concept of GNP, in measuring the value of the ultimate production of the economic system—that is, the total value of all goods and services enjoyed by its consumers or accumulated as new or replacement wealth. Hence we do not count the intermediate goods we have already noted in our economic panorama. To go back to an earlier example, we do not add up the value of the *cotton* and the *yarn* and the *cloth* and the final *clothing* when we compute the value of GNP. That kind of multiple counting might be very useful if we wanted certain information about our total economic activity, but it would not tell us accurately about the final value of output. For when we buy a shirt, the price we pay already includes the cost of the cloth to the shirtmaker; and in turn, the amount the shirtmaker paid for his cloth already included the cost of the yarn; and in turn, again, the seller of yarn included in his price the amount he

paid for raw cotton. Embodied in the price of the shirt, therefore, is the value of all the intermediate products that went into it. Thus in figuring the value for GNP, we add only the values of all final goods, both for consumption and for investment purposes.

2. *There are four categories of final goods.* In our first view of macroeconomic activity we divided the flow of output into two great streams: consumption and gross investment. Now, for purposes of a closer analysis, we impose a few refinements on this basic scheme.

First we must pay heed to a small flow of production that has previously escaped our notice. This is the net flow of goods or services that leaves this country; that is, the total flow going abroad minus the flow that enters. This international branch of our economy will play a relatively minor role in our analysis, and we will largely ignore it until Chapter 7. But we must give it its proper name: *net exports.* Because these net exports are a kind of investment (they are goods we produce but do not consume), we must now rename the great bulk of investment that remains in this country. We will henceforth formally call that *gross private domestic investment.*

The word *private* brings us to the second refinement. It concerns a subflow of goods and services within both the great consumption and the investment branches of over-all activity. These are the goods and services bought or produced by the government (as contrasted with consumers or businesses). Some of these goods may be in fact consumers' goods—policemen's services, for example—and some may be investment goods, such as roads or schools or dams. Conventionally, however, we include all public purchases, whether for consumption or investment, in a category called *government purchases of goods and services.*

In subsequent chapters we will become much more familiar with all of these flows of output, but it is well to make their acquaintance now. To recapitulate, we identify four kinds of final goods in the measurement of GNP:

Consumption goods and services

Gross private domestic investment

Government purchases of goods and services

Net exports

3. *GNP is not an exact measure.* Finally, a word of caution. We shall be dealing with and analyzing GNP throughout this book, but it is important to understand the weaknesses as well as the strengths of this most important of all economic indicators. To begin with, we must recognize that some items in GNP are much more exactly measureable than others. It is not too difficult to add up the sales value of the automobiles produced in the United States, but it is extremely difficult to compute accurately the value of the legal services rendered. Yet legal services enter into GNP, just as do auto sales.

Another statistical problem arises from the fact that items appear in GNP when they are bought on the marketplace, but disappear from the computation of GNP (even though they continue to exist) if they are obtained free. The work of domestic servants, for example, is counted in GNP as part of consumers' purchases of services, but the work of housewives is not. Thus, every time a man marries his cook, GNP declines by the amount of the wages that are no longer paid, even though the man continues to enjoy the services he once paid for.* Although the number of men who marry their cooks may be small, the number of people who live in their own houses (and who do not therefore pay rent) or who eat some food grown on their own farms (and who need not therefore buy all their food) is not small. These problems of *imputing* value-equivalents where services are produced and enjoyed but not paid for is a source of considerable complication in the computation of GNP.

Finally, there is the difficulty of reconciling dollar figures with whatever standards of value we wish to apply to a society. The greater or lesser care that parents bestow on their children, the quality of the entertainment represented by one million dollars worth of television entertainment and one million dollars worth of symphony admissions, the use or misuse made by consumers or businessmen or governments of their respective por-

---

* GNP declines even if he gives his wife an allowance equal to her former wage. Allowances are not presumed to measure "productive services," so they are not counted in GNP.

tions of total output—all these formidable problems of real life remain necessarily outside the pale of gross national product. GNP measures dollar figures of output as best it can, but it cannot measure the quality of life that those dollars represent.

Such problems lead economists to treat GNP with a certain gingerly respect—gingerly because the measure is, at best, highly approximative, and yet with respect because it remains the best single measure of economic performance that we possess. With that caution in mind, let us now proceed to an investigation of how GNP is generated and sustained.

# 3

# *Output and Income*

So far, we have talked about output as it emerges from the interaction of wealth and labor, but we have not inquired very deeply into the manner in which that interaction takes place. Yet the output of our economy does not spring forth "automatically" by the pursuit of changeless tradition, as is the case in simple pre-industrial societies. Nor is it brought into being because the labor force is more or less forcibly combined with material resources, as is the case in collectivized economics. Rather, as we have already mentioned, output results from innumerable activities and decisions on the marketplace where men buy and sell, largely as they wish. What we must now understand is precisely how this daily activity of the marketplace gives rise to the flow of gross national product.

## *Output and Demand*

How does the marketplace actually bring output into existence? How does it effect the combination of land, labor, and capital under the guidance of an entrepreneur? Any businessman will give you the answer. He will tell you the crucial factor enabling him to perform his microeconomic task (or in his language, "to run a business") is *demand;* that is, the presence of buyers who are willing and able to purchase some good or service at the price at which it is offered.

But how does demand come into being? How do the buyers in the marketplace get the dollars they use to induce sellers to produce goods and services? If we ask any buyer, he will tell you that his dollars come to him because they are part of his *income* or his cash receipts.

But where, in turn, do the dollar receipts or incomes of buyers come from? If we inquire again, most buyers will tell us that they have money in their pockets because in one fashion or another they have contributed to the process of production; that is, because they have helped to make the output that is now being sold.

Thus our quest for the motive force behind the flow of production leads us in a great circle through the market system. We can see this in the simple diagram below.

If we start at the top of the circle we find output resulting

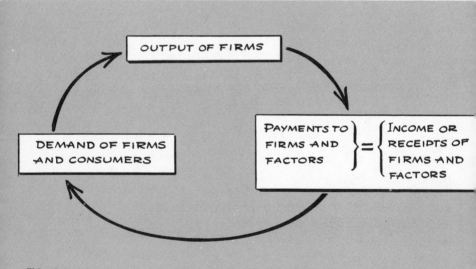

FIG. 3-1

*from* demand and in turn resulting *in* payments to firms or factors. Tracing the circle to the right, we see these payments, which are the incomes or receipts of factors and firms, become the basis for the market demand that is directed back to the original firms themselves.

## An Economic Model

We must examine this chain of payments and receipts in great detail, for it contains the key to the operation of our economic system. First, however, we need a word about our method of inquiry. It must be obvious that it is impossible to depict the flux of buying and selling as it actually occurs on the marketplace of the nation. It would require us to fix in our minds more details than can be reported on all the financial pages of all the newspapers in the nation every day. Hence, to comprehend the basic processes of the economy, we must use a special method of reducing its confusion to understandable dimensions. This we do by extracting from the actual happenings of economic life those aspects that experience and analysis have taught us to regard as central and critical. From these crucial links and processes we then create an imaginary *model* of an economy that exhibits, in its operation, all the essential movements of its real-life counterpart. We shall find our model to be an indispensable guide to the complicated reality of economic life around us.

Our model, to begin with, will be a very simple one. We must, of course, exclude from it all the variety of life itself: the differences in personality of one man and another, the peculiar ways that one market differs from another, the distinctions that separate one firm from its competitor. We reduce our economy, in other words, to a colorless and abstract reproduction of life in which we can speak of general kinds of relationships without having to qualify each and every statement to accommodate each and every existing situation. This ability—this necessity—to reduce the actual to the abstract is another aspect of the special intellectual demand that the economic view requires.

But our model will be simple not only in its disregard of "life." We must also simplify it, at first, by ruling out some of the very events to which we will later turn as the climax of our study. For instance, we shall ignore changes in people's tastes, so that we can assume that everyone will regularly buy the same kinds of goods. We shall ignore differences in the structure of firms or markets, so that we can forget about differences in competitive pressures. We shall rule out population growth and, even more important, inventive progress, so that we can deal with a very stable imaginary world. For the time being, we will exclude even saving and net investment (although of course we must permit replacement investment), so that we can ignore growth. Later, of course, we are to be deeply concerned with just such problems of dynamic change. But we shall not be able to come to grips with them until we have first understood an economic world as "pure" and changeless as possible.

## Cost and Output

We start, then, with an imaginary output, a gross national product that we shall picture as having emerged, all on the same day, from the farms and factories and offices where it was produced over the past year. If we like, we can think of it as sitting on the economic front doorstep looking for a buyer. What we must now see is whether it will be possible to *sell* this gross national product to the people who have been engaged in producing it. In other words, *we must ask whether there is enough income or receipts generated in the process of production to buy back all the products themselves.*

How does production create income? Businessmen do not think about "incomes" when they assemble the factors of production to meet the demand for their product. They worry about *cost*. All the money they pay out during the production process is paid under the heading of *cost*, whether it be wage or salary cost, cost of materials, depreciation cost, tax cost, or whatever. Thus it would seem that the concept of cost may offer us a useful point of entry into the economic chain. For if we can show how costs can become incomes, we will have taken a major step toward understanding whether our gross national product can in fact be sold to those who produced it.

## A Cost Summary

It may help us if we begin by looking at the kinds of costs incurred by business firms in real life. Here is a hypothetical expense summary of General Manufacturing for 1963, which will serve as an example typical of all business firms, large or small.

**GENERAL MANUFACTURING**
Cost summary

| | |
|---|---|
| Wages, salaries, and employee benefits | $100,000,000 |
| Rental, interest, and profits payments | 5,000,000 |
| Materials, supplies, etc. | 50,000,000 |
| Taxes other than income | 15,000,000 |
| Depreciation | 20,000,000 |

## Factor Costs and National Income

Some of these costs we recognize immediately as payments to factors of production. The item for "wages and salaries" is obviously a payment to the factor *labor*. The item interest (perhaps not so obviously) is a payment to the factor *capital*—that is, to those who have lent the company money in order to help it carry on its productive operation. The item for rent is, of course, a payment for the rental of *land* or resources from their owners.

Note that we have included profits with rent and interest. In actual accounting practice, profits are not shown as an expense, and if we were going into complex microtheory, we should have a good deal to say about the meaning of profits. For our purposes, however, it will be quite legitimate and very helpful to regard profits as a special kind of factor cost going to entrepreneurs for their risk-taking function. In our next chapter, we shall go a little more thoroughly into the matter of profits.

Two things strike us about these factor costs. First, it is clear that they represent payments that have been made to secure production. In more technical language, they are payments for factor inputs that result in commodity outputs. All the production actually carried on within the company, all the value it has added to the economy, has been compensated by the payments the company has made to land, labor, and capital. To be sure, the company has incurred other costs, for materials and taxes and depreciation, and we shall soon turn to these. But whatever production, or assembly, or distribution the company itself has carried out during the course of the year has required the use of land, labor, or capital. Thus the *total of its factor costs represents the value of the total new output that General Manufacturing by itself has given to the economy.*

From here it is but a simple step to add up *all* the factor costs paid out by *all* the companies in the economy, in order to measure the total new value added by *all* productive efforts in the year. This measure is called *national income* (or sometimes national income at factor cost).* As we can see, it is less than gross national product, for it does not include other costs of output; namely, certain taxes and depreciation.

## Factor Costs and Household Incomes

A second fact that strikes us is that *factor costs are income payments.* The wages, salaries, interest, rents, etc., that were costs to the company were income to its recipients. So are the profits, which will accrue to the owners of the business.

Thus, just as it sounds, *national income* means the total amount of earnings of the factors of production within the nation. If we think of these factors as constituting the households of the economy, we can see that factor costs result directly in incomes to the *household sector.* Thus, if factor costs were the only costs involved in production, the problem of buying back the gross national product would be a very simple one. We should simply be paying out to households, as the cost of production, the very sum needed to buy GNP when we turned around to sell it.

---

* It might be well to add that not all production (and therefore not all national income) originates with companies. Governments also produce value, such as the output of firemens' services or of roads, and private individuals, like farmers or doctors, produce output as "proprietorships." For the purposes of exposition, however, we can think of government units or individual proprietorships as "companies" since they incur exactly the same kinds of costs.

But this is not the case, as a glance at the General Manufacturing expense summary shows. There are other costs, besides factor costs. How shall we deal with them?

## Costs of Materials

The next item on the expense summary is puzzling. Called payments for "materials, supplies, etc.," it represents all the money General Manufacturing has paid, not to its own factors, but to other companies for other products it has needed. We may even recognize these costs as payments for those intermediate products that lose their identity in a later stage of production. How do such payments become part of the income available to buy GNP on the marketplace?

Perhaps the answer is already intuitively clear. When the General Manufacturing sends its checks to, let us say, U.S. Steel, or General Electric, or to a local supplier of stationery, each of these recipient firms now uses the proceeds of General Manufacturing's checks to pay its own costs. (Actually, of course, they have probably long since paid their own costs and now use General Manufacturing's payment only to reimburse themselves. But if we want to picture our model economy in the simplest way, we can imagine U.S. Steel and other firms sending their products to General Manufacturing and waiting until checks arrive to pay their own costs.)

And what are those costs? What must U.S. Steel or all the other suppliers now do with their checks? The answer is obvious. They must now reimburse their own factors and then pay any other costs that remain.

The next diagram may make the matter plain. It shows us, looking back down the chain of intermediate payments, that what constitutes material costs to one firm is made up of factor and other costs to another. Indeed, as we unravel the chain from company to company, it is clear that all the contribution to new output must have come from the contribution of factors somewhere down the line, and that all the costs of new output—all the value added—must be resolvable into payments to land, labor, and capital.

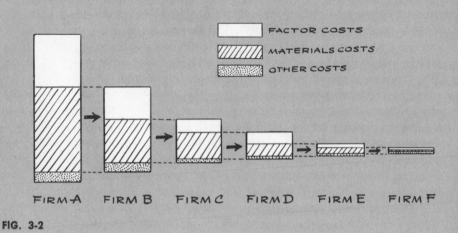

FIG. 3-2

Another way of picturing the same thing is to imagine that all firms in the country were bought up by a single gigantic corporation. The various production units of the new supercorporation would then ship components and semifinished items back and forth to one another, but there would not have to be any payment from one division to another. The only payments that would be necessary would be those required to buy the services of factors—that is, various kinds of labor, or the use of property or capital—so that at the end of the year, the supercorporation would show on its expense summary only items for wages and salaries, rent, and interest (and as we shall see, taxes and depreciation) but it would have no item for materials cost.

## Other Costs

We have come a bit further toward seeing how our gross national product can be sold. To the extent that GNP represents new output made during the course of the year, the income to buy back this output has already been handed out as factor costs, either paid at the last stage of production or "carried along" in the guise of materials costs. But a glance at the General Manu-facturing expense summary shows that entrepreneurs incur two kinds of costs that we have still not taken into account: taxes and depreciation. Here are costs employers have incurred that have not been accounted for on the income side. What can we say about them?

## Tax Costs

Let us begin by tracing the taxes that General Manufactur-ing pays, just as we have traced its materials payments. In the first instance, its taxes will go to government units—federal, state, and local. But we need not stop there. Just as we saw that Gen-eral Manufacturing's checks to supplier firms paid for the sup-pliers' factor costs and for still further interfirm transactions, so we can see that its checks to government agencies pay for goods and services that these agencies have bought—goods such as roads, buildings, or defense equipment; or services such as teaching, police protection, and the administration of justice. General Manufacturing's tax checks are thus used to help pay for factors of production—land, labor, and capital—that are used in the *pub-lic sector.*

In many ways, General Manufacturing's payments to govern-ment units resemble its payments to other firms for raw ma-terials. Indeed, if the government *sold* its output to General Manufacturing, charging for the use of the roads, police services, or defense protection it affords the company, there would be *no* difference whatsoever. The reason we differentiate between a company's payment to the public sector and its payments for intermediate products is important, however, and worth looking into.

The first reason is clearly that, with few exceptions, the gov-ernment does *not* sell its output. This is partly because the com-munity has decided that certain things the government produces (education, justice, or the use of public parks, for instance) should not be for sale but should be supplied to all citizens with-out charge. In part, it is also because some things the government produces, such as defense or law and order, cannot be equitably charged to individual buyers, since it is impossible to say to what degree anyone benefits from—or even uses—these communal facilities. Hence General Manufacturing, like every other producer, is billed, justly or otherwise, for a share of the cost of government.

## Direct Taxes

There is also a second reason why we consider the cost of taxes as a new kind of cost, distinct from factor payments. It is that when we have finished paying the factors we have not yet paid all the sums that employers must lay out. Some taxes, in other words, are an addition to the cost of production.

Note that not all taxes collected by the government are costs of production. Many taxes will be paid, not by the entrepreneurs as an expense of doing business, but by the *factors* themselves. These so-called *direct* taxes (such as income taxes) are *not* part of the cost of production. When we tax a worker's or a stockholder's income, we do not add that tax back onto the costs of the firm. Such direct taxes only transfer income from earners to government hands. We shall hear more about these transfers in our next chapter.

In the same way, the income taxes on the profits of a company do *not* constitute a cost of production. General Manufacturing does not pay income taxes as a regular charge on its operations, but waits until a year's production has taken place, and then pays income taxes on the profits it makes *after* paying its costs. If it finds that it has lost money over the year, it will not pay any income taxes—although it will have paid other costs, including certain other kinds of taxes. Thus direct taxes are not a cost that is paid out in the course of production, and must be recouped, but a payment made by factors (including owners of the business) from the incomes they have earned through the process of production.

## Indirect Taxes

But we are not done with taxes. Even though direct taxes, on the factors themselves or on the profits of enterprise, are not costs of production, there are some taxes that are costs of production. These taxes—so-called *indirect taxes*—are levied directly on the productive enterprise itself or on its actual physical output, and not on the incomes of the factors or the income of the company that belongs to the factors. Taxes on real estate, for instance, or taxes that are levied on each unit of output, regardless of whether it is sold at a profit (such as cigarette excise taxes), or taxes levied on goods sold at retail (sales taxes) are all payments that entrepreneurs must make merely for the privilege of doing business.

Thus we can see two reasons why taxes are handled as a separate item in GNP and are not telescoped into factor costs, the way materials costs are. One reason is that taxes are a payment to a *different sector* from that of business and thus indicate a separate stream of economic activity. But the second reason, and the one that interests us more at this moment, is that *certain taxes—* indirect taxes—*are an entirely new kind of cost of production, not previously picked up.* As an expense paid out by entrepreneurs, over and above factor costs (or materials costs), these tax costs must be part of the total selling price of GNP.

Will there be enough incomes handed out in the process of production to cover this item of cost?

We have seen that there will be. The tax costs paid out by entrepreneurs will be received by government agencies who will use their tax receipts to pay incomes to factors working for the government, or to pay firms who provide goods to the government. Thus the new item of tax costs will eventually become income to factors working in the public sector, and will be available, together with all other factor incomes, to create demand on the marketplace.

### Depreciation

But there is still one last item of cost. At the end of the year, when the company is toting up its expenses to see if it has made a profit for the year, its accountants do not stop with factor costs, material costs, and taxes. If they did, the company would soon be in serious straits. In producing its goods, General Manufacturing has also used up a certain amount of its assets—its buildings and equipment—and a cost must now be charged for this wear and tear if the company is to be able to preserve the value of its physical plant intact. If it did not make this cost allowance, it would have failed to include all the resources that were used up in the process of production, and it would therefore be over-stating its profits.

Yet, this cost has something about it clearly different from the other costs General Manufacturing has paid. Unlike factor costs, or taxes, or materials costs, the company does not have to send anybody a check when its accountants make an allowance for depreciation. In fact, all they do is to make an entry on the company's books, stating that plant and equipment are now worth so-and-so much less than in the beginning of the year.

At the same time however, General Manufacturing *includes* the amount of depreciation in the price it intends to charge for its goods. As we have seen, part of the resources used up in pro-duction was its own capital equipment, and it is certainly en-titled to consider the depreciation as a cost. Yet, it has not paid anyone a sum of money equal to this cost! How, then, will there be enough income in the marketplace to buy back its product?

The answer takes us out of the immediate present, to some time in the past—say the beginning of the production year—when General Manufacturing and other companies installed or built their present equipment. At that time they *did* pay out incomes to other firms who put up their plant or sold them their ma-chines, and these other firms, needless to say, used their receipts to pay their own factors, taxes, and other expenses. Thus an amount of expenditure equivalent to the value of plant and equipment that is now being depreciated *has already been paid out and is already in the hands of buyers.*

Now, however, we seem to be in a different fix. Suppose the plant and equipment of the company cost $200 million, and that each year 10 per cent of its costs are written off as depreciation. Then it would seem that $200 million in purchasing power must have been paid out in the past, whereas only $20 million of depreciation is being added on as this year's cost. Suddenly we have too much purchasing power, not too little!

To clear up the dilemma, we must remind ourselves once again that we look down, not merely upon one company, but on a society composed of a huge number of companies. If we assume that these companies have built their capital assets in various years, we can see how a balance could be worked out between depreciation charges and expenditures for replacement equipment. Each year *all* companies would add to their costs a regular amount for depreciation. At the same time *some* companies would actually be ordering replacement equipment.

This clarifies the question that originally puzzled us. For we can now see that insofar as there is a steady stream of expenditure going to firms that make replacement capital, there will be payments just large enough to balance the marking-up of costs due to depreciation. As with all other payments to firms, these replacement expenditures will, of course, become incomes to factors, etc., and thus can reappear on the marketplace.*

## *The Three Streams of Expenditure*

Our analysis is now essentially complete. Item by item, we have traced each element of cost into an income payment, so that we now know there is enough income paid out to buy back our GNP at a price that represents its full cost.

Perhaps this was a conclusion we anticipated all along. After all, ours would be an impossibly difficult economy to manage if somewhere along the line purchasing power dropped out of existence, so that we were always faced with a shortage of income to buy back the product we made. But our analysis has also shown us a most unexpected thing. We are accustomed to thinking that all the purchasing power in the economy is received and spent through the hands of "people"—by which we usually mean households. Now we can see that this is not true. There is not only one, but there are *three* streams of incomes and costs, all

---

* We should note, however, that replacement expenditures may *not* be spaced regularly—or they may not be made at all!—so that the return of depreciation accruals via replacement expenditures may be bumpy rather than smooth. We shall have much more to say about this when we reach our chapter on investment. At this point we want only to understand how costs *can be* (and in fact usually are) returned to the marketplace.

quite distinct from one another. One of these is the factor–household–consumers goods stream. Another is the tax–government agency–government goods stream. A third is the depreciation–business–replacement stream.

To help visualize these three flows, imagine for an instant that our money comes in colors (all of equal value): green, red, and blue. Now suppose that firms always pay their factors in green money, their taxes in red money, and their replacement expenditures in blue money. In point of fact, of course, the colors would soon be mixed. A factor paid in green bills will be paying some of his green income for taxes; or a government agency will be paying out red money as factor incomes; or firms will be using blue dollars to pay taxes or factors, and red or green dollars to pay for replacement capital.

But at least in our mind we could picture the streams being kept quite separate. A red tax dollar paid by General Manufacturing to the Internal Revenue Service for taxes could go from the government to another firm, let us say in payment for office supplies, and we can think of the office supply firm keeping these red dollars apart from its other receipts, to pay its taxes with. Such a red dollar could circulate indefinitely, helping to bring about production but never entering a consumer's pocket! In the same way, a blue replacement expenditure dollar going from General Manufacturing to, let us say U.S. Steel, could be set aside by U.S. Steel to pay for *its* replacement needs; and the firm that received this blue dollar might, in turn, set it aside for its own use as replacement expenditure.

There is a simple way of explaining this seemingly complex triple flow. Each stream indicates the existence of a *final taker* of gross national product: consumers, government, and business itself.* Since output has final claimants other than consumers, we can obviously have a flow of purchasing power that does not enter consumers' or factors' hands.

* We continue to forget about net exports until Chapter 7. We can think of them perfectly satisfactorily as a component of gross private investment.

## The Crucial Role of Expenditures

The realization that factors do not gét paid incomes equal to the total gross value of output brings us back to the central question of this chapter: can we be certain that we will be able to sell our GNP at its full cost? Has there surely been generated enough purchasing power to buy back our total output?

We have thus far carefully analyzed and answered half the question. *We know that all costs will become incomes to factors or receipts of government agencies or of firms making replacement items.* To sum up again, factor costs become the incomes of workers, managements, owners of natural resources and of capital; and all these incomes together can be thought of as comprising the receipts of the household sector. Tax costs are paid to government agencies and become receipts of the government sector. Depreciation costs are initially accrued within business firms, and these accruals belong to the business sector. If worn-out capital is regularly replaced, these accruals will then be matched by equivalent new receipts of capital-goods-making firms.

What we have not yet established, however, is that these sector receipts will become sector *expenditures*. That is, we have not demonstrated that all households will now *spend* all their incomes on goods and services, or that government units will necessarily *spend* all their tax receipts on public goods and services, or that all firms will assuredly *spend* their depreciation accruals for new replacement equipment.

What happens if some receipts are not spent? The answer is of key importance in understanding the operation of the economy. A failure of the sectors to spend as much money as they have received means that some of the costs that have been laid out will *not* come back to the original entrepreneurs. As a result, they will suffer losses. If, for instance, our gross national product cost $600 billion to produce, but if the various sectors in all spent only $590 billion, then some entrepreneurs would find themselves failing to sell all their output, or having to sell it at a price below cost. Business firms would report losses, and they would try to save money wherever they could. The easiest way to save money is to spend less, perhaps by firing some employees, or by failing to replace worn-out capital goods. As a result, costs would go down, but so would incomes and receipts, for we have seen that costs and incomes are but opposite sides of one coin. As incomes fall, the expenditures of the sectors might very well fall further, bringing about another twist in the spiral of recession.

This is not yet the place to go into the mechanics of such a downward spiral of business. But the point is clear. *A failure of the sectors to bring all their receipts back to the marketplace as demand can initiate profound economic problems.* In the contrast between an unshakeable equality of costs and incomes on the one hand, and the uncertain connection between receipts and expenditures on the other, we have come to grips with one of the most important problems in macroeconomics.

## The Complete Circuit

We shall have ample opportunity later to observe exactly what happens when receipts are not spent. Now let us be sure that we understand how the great circle of the economic flow is closed when the sectors *do* spend their receipts. The diagram opposite shows how we can trace our "red, blue, and green" dollars through the economy and how these flows suffice to buy back GNP for its total cost.

We can trace the flow from left to right. We begin on the left with the bar representing the total cost of our freshly produced GNP. As we know, this cost consists of all the factor costs of all the firms and government units in the nation, all the indirect tax costs incurred during production, and all the depreciation charges made during production. The bar also shows us the amount of money demand our economy must generate in order to buy back its own output.

The next bars show us the transmutation of costs into sector receipts for householders, government units, and business firms (who retain their own depreciation accruals). This relationship between costs and sector receipts is one of *identity*—all costs

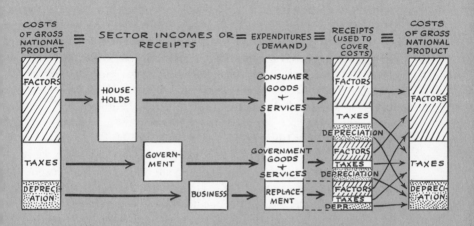

FIG. 3-3

*must* be receipts. Hence we use the sign ≡ to indicate that this is a relation of identities—of definitional differences only.

Thereafter we notice the crucial link. Each sector dutifully spends all its receipts, as it is supposed to. Our household sector buys the kinds of goods and services householders do in fact buy—consumption goods and services. Our government sector buys government goods and services, and our business sector buys replacement investment. This time we use an equals sign (=) because this is emphatically *not* a relationship of identity.

Now note the next bar. Here we see what happens to these expenditures when they are received by the firms who make consumer goods, or by the firms or individuals who make goods and services bought by governments, or by the manufacturers of capital equipment. Each of these recipients will use the money he has received to cover factor payments, taxes, and depreciation for his own business. (What we show in our diagram are not these costs for each and every firm, but the aggregate costs for all firms selling to each sector.)

We are almost done. It remains only to aggregate the sector costs; that is, to add up all the factor costs, all the taxes, and all the depreciation accruals of *all* firms and government agencies—to reproduce a bar just like the one we started with. A circle of production has been completed. Firms and government units have received back on the marketplace a sum just large enough to cover their initial costs, including their profits for risk. The stage is set for another round of production, similar to the last.

### Gross National Product, Net National Product, National Income

Our bar graph also enables us to examine again the concept of gross national product, for now we can see that GNP can be looked at in one of two ways, which add up to the same thing. One conception of GNP is a *sum of costs*—factor costs, indirect taxes, and depreciation—that were incurred in the production of the nation's final output. The other conception of GNP is a *sum of expenditures* on this same final output; that is, consumption expenditure, government expenditure, and gross private investment expenditure. Since the final output is one and the same, we can see that these two ways of computing its value must be the same, too. One method merely separates total output into various categories of cost, while the other tells us who bought the output as it finally emerged.*

It is now also very easy to understand the meaning of two other, less frequently used measures of output. One of these is called *net national product* (NNP). As the name indicates, it is exactly equal to gross national product *minus depreciation*. The other measure, national income, we have already met. It is GNP *minus depreciation and indirect taxes*. This makes it equal to the sum of factor costs only. The following diagram should make this relationship clear.

---

* And what if no one bought it? Then it will pile up in warehouses as inventories and will count as investment—although, in this case, very unwanted investment. More about this later.

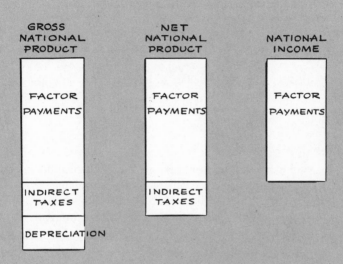

**FIG. 3-4**

*The Circular Flow*

The "self-reproducing" model economy we have now sketched out is obviously still very far from reality. Nevertheless, the particular kind of unreality that we have deliberately constructed serves a highly useful purpose. An economy that regularly and dependably buys back everything it produces gives us a kind of bench mark from which to begin our subsequent investigations. We call such an economy, whose internal relationships we have outlined, an economy in *stationary equilibruim,* and we denote the changeless flow of costs into business receipts and receipts back into costs a *circular flow.*

We shall return many times to the model of a circular flow economy for insights into a more complex and dynamic system. Hence it is well that we summarize briefly two of the salient characteristics of such a system.

1. *A circular flow economy will never experience a "recession."* Year in and year out, its total output will remain unchanged. Indeed, the very concept of a circular flow is useful in showing us that an economic system can maintain a given level of activity *indefinitely,* so long as all the sectors convert all their receipts into expenditure.\*

2. *A circular flow economy also will never know a "boom."* That is, it will not grow, and its standard of living will remain unchanged. That standard of living may be high or low, for we could have a circular flow economy of poverty or of abundance. But in either state, changelessness will be of its essence.

In the chapters that follow, we must successively reintroduce the very elements that we have so carefully excluded. First, saving and net investment, then technological change and population growth must one by one find their way back into our model. Thus, gradually it will approximate itself to the realities around us, allowing us to return from the abstract world of ideas to the concrete world of reality.

\* And so long as we have no technological change, which we have thus far ruled out of our model.

# 4

# Saving and Investment

Let us return for a moment to our original perspective overlooking the economic flow. We will remember that we could see the workings of the economy as an interaction between the factors of production and their environment, culminating in a stream of production—some private, some public—that was used in part for consumption and in part for the replacement or the further building up of capital. Now in our model of a circular flow economy we have seen how such an economy can be self-sustaining and self-renewing, as each round of disbursements by employers found its way into a stream of purchasing power just large enough to justify the continuation of the given scale of output.

## The Meaning of Saving

Yet we all know that such a circular flow is a highly unreal depiction of the world. Indeed, it omits the most important dynamic factor of real economic life—the steady accumulation of new capital (and the qualitative change in the nature of the capital due to technology) that characterizes a *growing* economy. What we must now investigate is the process by which society

43

adds each year to its stock of real wealth—and the effect of this process on the circuit of production and purchasing.

We begin by making sure that we understand a key word in this dynamic analysis—*saving*. In Chapter 2, we spoke of saving as the act by which society relinquishes resources that might have been used for consumption, thereby making them available for the capital-building stream of output. Now we must translate that underlying, real meaning of saving into terms corresponding with the buying and selling, paying and receiving discussed in the preceding chapter.

What is saving in these terms? It is very simply *not spending all or part of income for consumption goods or services.** It should be very clear then why saving is such a key term. In our discussion of the circular flow, it became apparent that expenditure was the critical link in the steady operation of the economy. If saving is not-spending, then it would seem that saving could be the cause for just that kind of downward spiral of which we caught a glimpse in our preceding chapter.

And yet this clearly is not the whole story. We also know that the act of investing—of spending money to direct factors into the production of capital goods—requires an act of saving—that is, of not using that same money to direct those factors instead into the production of consumers goods. *Hence, saving is clearly necessary for the process of investment or growth.* Now, how can one and the same act be necessary for economic expansion and a threat to its stability? This is a problem that will occupy us during much of this book.

## The Demand Gap

It will help us to understand the problem if we again have recourse to our now familiar diagram of the circular flow. But this time we must introduce into it the crucial new fact of net

---

* Note "for consumption goods and services." Purchasing stocks or bonds or life insurance is also an act of saving, even though you must spend money to acquire these items. What you acquire, however, are assets, not consumption goods and services. Some acts of spending are difficult to classify. Is a college education, for instance, a consumption good or an investment? It is probably better thought of as an investment—but in the statistics of GNP it is treated as consumption.

saving. Note *net* saving. Quite unnoticed, we have already encountered gross saving in our circular flow, together with gross investment. After all, in our model economy, replacement expenditures for capital goods used money that might have been paid out to stockholders or workers. Thus there was a regular not-spending on the part of businesses (whose owners might have taken the depreciation accruals as part of their own income), offset by an equally regular spending for replacement investment. But this saving did not buy *additional* capital; it merely replaced worn-out equipment with identical new equipment. That is why we call it gross saving, rather than net.

In this look at our model economy, however, we assume that when employers pay out their factor costs, householders will save a portion of their incomes. The result is shown in Fig. 4-1.

What we see is precisely what we would expect. There is a gap in demand introduced by the deficiency of consumer spending. This means that the total receipts of employers who make consumer goods will be less than the total amounts they laid

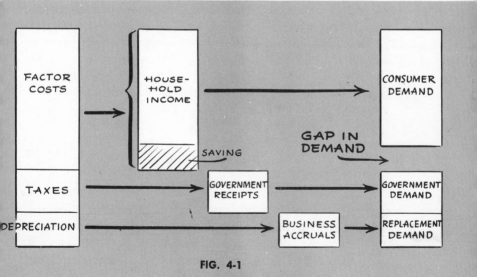

**FIG. 4-1**

out. It begins to look as if we were approaching the cause of economic recession and unemployment.

Yet, whereas we have introduced saving, we have forgotten about its counterpart, investment. Cannot the investment activity of a growing economy in some way close the demand gap?

### The Dilemma of Saving

This is indeed, as we shall soon see, the way out of the dilemma. But before we trace the way in which investment compensates for saving, let us draw two conclusions from the analysis we have made up to this point.

1. The act of saving, in and by itself, creates a gap in demand, a shortage of spending. Unless this gap is closed, there will be trouble in the economic system, for employers will not be getting back as receipts all the sums they laid out.

2. The presence of a demand gap forces us to make a choice. If we want a dynamic, investing economy, we will have to be prepared to cope with the problems that saving raises. If we want to avoid these problems, we can close the gap by urging consumers not to save. Then we would have a dependable circular flow, but we would no longer enjoy economic growth.

### The Offset to Savings

How, then, shall we manage to make our way out of the dilemma of saving? The previous diagram makes clear what must be done. If a gap in demand is due to the savings of households, then that gap must be closed by the expanded spending of some other sector. There are only two other such sectors: government or business. Thus in some fashion or other, the savings of one sector must be "offset" by the increased activity of another.

But how is this offset to take place? How are the resources that are relinquished by consumers to be made available to entrepreneurs in the business sector or to government officials? In a market economy there is only one way that resources or factors not being used in one place can be used in another. Someone must be willing and able to hire them.

Whether or not government and business are willing to employ the factors that are not needed in the consumer goods sector is a very critical matter, soon to command much of our attention. But suppose that they *are* willing. How will they be able to do so? How can they get the necessary funds to expand their activity?

There are four principal methods of accomplishing this essential increase in expenditure.

1. The business sector can increase its expenditures by *borrowing* the savings of the public through the sale of new corporate bonds.

2. The government sector can increase its expenditures by *borrowing* savings from the other sectors through the sale of new government bonds.

3. The business sector can increase its expenditures by attracting household savings into partnerships, new stock, or other *ownership or equity*.

4. Both business and government sectors can increase expenditures by *borrowing* additional funds from commercial banks.

There are other possibilities. Government has a very important means of increasing its command over resources, through taxing the household or business sectors (although in this case it is not always clear whether the government is acquiring funds that would have been saved, or merely forcing other sectors to give up funds that they might have spent). Business can also increase its expenditures by using its own savings to finance new spending.

## Claims

But the four important methods itemized above all have one attribute that calls them especially to our attention. Without exception they give rise to *claims* that reveal from whom the funds have been obtained and to whom they have been made available, as well as on what terms. Bonds, corporate or government, show that savings have been borrowed from individuals or banks by business and government units. Shares of stock reveal that savings have been obtained on an equity (ownership) basis, as do new partnership agreements.

We can note a few additional points about claims, now that we see how many of them arise in the economy. First, many household savings are first put into banks and insurance companies—so-called financial intermediaries—so that the transfer of funds from households to business or government may go through several stages; e.g., from household to insurance company and then from insurance company to corporation.

Second, not *all* claims involve the offsetting of savings of one sector by expenditures of another. Many claims, once they have arisen, are traded back and forth and bought and sold, as is the case with most stocks and bonds. These purchases and sales involve the *transfer of* existing claims, not the creation of new claims.

Finally, not every new claim necessarily involves the creation of an asset. If A borrows $5 from B, bets it on the races, and gives B his note, there has been an increase in claims, but no new asset has been brought into being to match it.

## Public and Private Claims

Now let us look at the next diagram. This time we show what happens when savings are made available to the business sector by direct borrowing from households. Note the claim (or equity) that arises.

If the government were doing the borrowing, rather than the business sector, the diagram would look like Fig. 4-3. Notice that the claim is now a government bond.

We have not looked at a diagram showing business or government borrowing its funds from the banking system. This process will be better understood when we take up the problem of money and banking, in Chapter 9. The basic concept, however, although more complex, is much the same as above.

## The Completed Act of Offsetting Savings

There remains only a last step, which must by now be fully anticipated. We have seen how it is possible to offset the savings in one sector, where they were going to cause an expenditure gap,

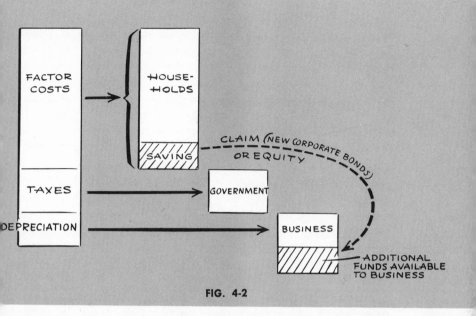

**FIG. 4-2**

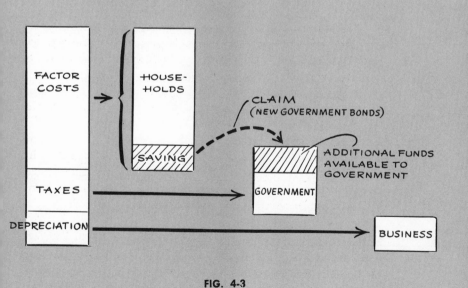

**FIG. 4-3**

by increasing the funds available to another sector. It remains only to *spend* those additional funds in the form of additional investment or, in the case of the government, for additional public goods and services. The two completed expenditure circuits now appear in Fig. 4-4, opposite.

### Intersectoral Offsets

We shall not investigate further at this point the differences between increased public spending and increased business investment. What we must heed is the crucial point at issue: *if saving in any one sector is to be offset, some other sector (or sectors) must spend more than its income. A gap in demand due to insufficient expenditure in one sector can be compensated only by an increase in demand—that is, in expenditure—of another.*

Once this simple but fundamental point is clearly understood, much of the mystery of macroeconomics disappears, for we can then begin to see that an economy in movement, as contrasted with one in a stationary circular flow, is one in which sectors must *cooperate* to maintain the closed circuit of income and output. In a dynamic economy, we no longer enjoy the steady translation of incomes into expenditure which, as we have seen, is the key to an uninterrupted flow of output. Rather, we are faced with the presence of net saving and the possibility of a gap in final demand. Difficult though the ensuing problems are, let us not forget that saving is the necessary condition for the accumulation of capital. The price of economic growth, in other words, is the risk of economic decline.

### Real and Financial Saving

This central importance of saving in a growing economy will become a familiar problem. At this juncture, where we have first encountered the difficulties it can pose, we must be certain that we understand two different aspects that saving assumes.

One aspect, noticed in our initial overview of the economy, is the decision to relinquish *resources* that can then be redeployed into capital-building. This is the real significance of saving. But this "real" aspect of saving is not the way we en-

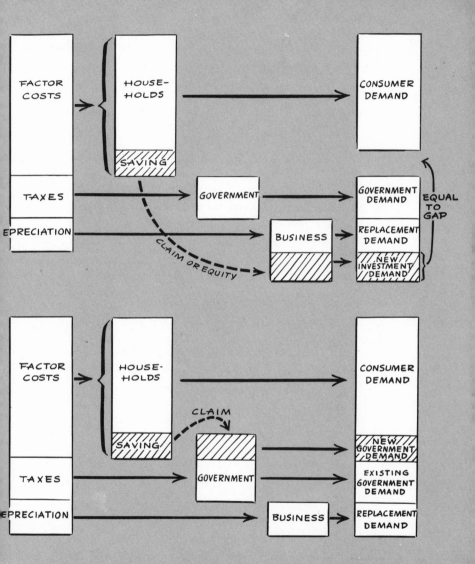

**FIG. 4-4**

counter the act of saving in our ordinary lives. We think of saving as a monetary phenomenon, not a "real" one. When we save, we are conscious of not using all our incomes for consumption, but we scarcely, if ever, think of releasing resources for alternative employments.

There is a reason for this dichotomy of real and financial saving. In our society, with its extraordinary degree of specialization, the individuals or institutions that do the actual saving are not ordinarily those who do the actual capital-building. In a simple society, this dichotomy between saving and investing need not, and usually does not, occur. A farmer who decides to build new capital—for example, to build a barn—is very much aware of giving up a consumption activity—the raising of food—in order to carry out his investment. So is an artisan who stops weaving clothing to repair his loom. Where the saver and the investor are one and the same person, there need be no "financial" saving, and the underlying real phenomenon of saving as the diversion of activity from consumption to investment is immediately apparent.

In the modern world, savers and investors are sometimes the same individual or group—as in the case of a business management that spends profits on new productive capacity rather than on higher executive salaries. More often, however, savers are not investors. Certainly householders, though very important savers, do not personally decide and direct the process of capital formation in the nation. Furthermore, the men and materials that households voluntarily relinquish by not using all their incomes to buy consumers goods have to be physically transferred to different industries, often to different occupations and locations, in order to carry out their investment tasks. This requires funds in the hands of the investors, so that they can tempt resources from one use to another.

Hence we need an elaborate system by which financial saving can be "transferred" directly or indirectly into the hands of those who will be in a position to employ factors for capital construction purposes. Nevertheless, underlying this complex mechanism for transferring purchasing power remains the same simple pur-

pose that we initially witnessed. Resources that have been relinquished from the production of consumption goods or services
are now employed in the production of capital goods. Thus,
*saving and investing are essentially real phenomena,* even though
it may take a great deal of financial manipulation to bring them
about.

A final point. The fact that the *decisions* to save and the
*decisions* to invest are lodged in different individuals or groups
alerts us to a basic reason why the savings–investment process
may not always work smoothly. Savers may choose to consume
less than their total incomes at times when investors have no
interest in expanding their capital assets. Alternatively, business
firms may wish to form new capital when savers are interested in
spending money only on themselves. This separation of decision-
making can give rise to situations in which savings are not offset
by investment, or in which investment plans race out ahead of
savings capabilities. In our next chapters we will be investigating
what happens in these cases.

### Transfer Payments

We have talked about the transfer of purchasing power from
savers to investors, but we have not yet mentioned another kind
of transfer, also of great importance in the over-all operation of
the economy. This is the transfer of incomes from sector to sector
(and sometimes within sectors).

Income transfers (called *transfer payments*) are a very useful
and important means of reallocating purchasing power in society. Through transfer payments, members of the community
who do not participate in production are given an opportunity
to enjoy incomes that would otherwise not be available to them.
Thus Social Security transfer payments make it possible for the
old or the handicapped to be given an "income" (not, to be sure
a currently *earned* income) of their own, or unemployment benefits give purchasing power to those who cannot get it through
employment.

Not all transfers are in the nature of welfare payments, however. The distribution of money *within* a household is a transfer

payment. So is the payment of interest on the national debt.* So is the grant of a subsidy to a private enterprise, such as an airline, or of a scholarship to a college student. Any income payment that is not earned by selling one's productive services on the market falls in the transfer category.

It may help to understand this process if we visualize it in our flow diagram. Figure 4-5 shows two kinds of transfers. The upper one, from the government to the household sector, shows a typical transfer of incomes, such as veterans' pensions or Social Security; the transfer below it reflects the flow of income that might be illustrated by a payment to agriculture for crop support. Transfers *within* sectors, such as household allowances, are not shown in the diagram.

One thing we may well note about transfers is that they can

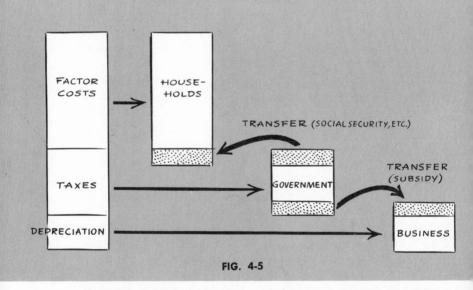

**FIG. 4-5**

---

* Curiously, the payment of interest on corporate debt is not considered a transfer payment, but a payment to a factor of production. Actually, much government interest should also be thought of as a factor payment (for the loan of capital for purposes of public output); but by convention, all government interest is classified as a transfer payment.

only rearrange the incomes created in the production process; they cannot increase those incomes. Income, as we learned in the last chapter, is inextricably tied to output—indeed, income is only the financial counterpart of output.

Transfer payments, on the other hand, are a way of arranging individual claims to production in some fashion that strikes the community as fairer or more efficient or more decorous than the way the market process allocates them through the production process. As such, transfer payments are an indispensable and often invaluable agency of social policy. But it is important to understand that no amount of transfers can, in itself, increase the total that is to be shared. That can happen only by raising output itself.

## Transfer Payments and Taxes

We have mentioned, but only in passing, another means of transferring purchasing power from one sector to another: taxation. Heretofore, however, we have often spoken as though all government tax receipts were derived from indirect taxes that were added onto the cost of production.

In fact, this is not the only source of government revenue. Indirect taxes are an important part of state and local revenues, but they are only a minor part of federal tax receipts. Most federal taxes are levied on the incomes of the factors of production or on the profits of businesses after the other factors have been paid.

Once again it is worth remembering that the government taxes consumers (and businesses) because it is in the nature of much government output that it cannot be *sold*. Taxes are the way we are billed for our share—rightly or wrongly figured—of the government activity that has been collectively decided upon. As we can now see, taxes—both on business and on the household sector—also finance many transfer payments. That is, the government intervenes in the distribution process to make it conform to our politically expressed social purposes, taking away some incomes from certain individuals and groups, and providing incomes to others. Figure 4-6 shows what this looks like in the GNP-creating process.

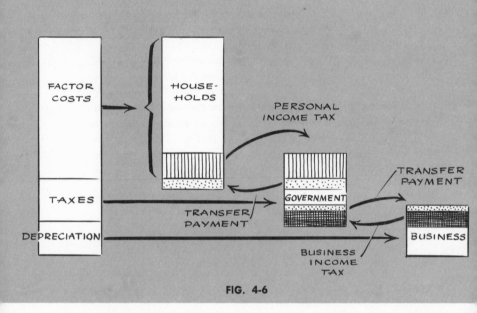

**FIG. 4-6**

As we can see, the exchanges of income between the household and the government sectors can be very complex. Income can flow from households to government units via taxation, and return to the household sector via transfer payments; and the same two-way flows can take place between government and business.

### Profits and Savings

In Chapter 8, we shall come back to the question of transfers. Now, one more important aspect of reality must now be introduced into our discussion. This is the role of profits in the savings–investment process.

During our discussion of the circular flow, we spoke of profits as a special kind of factor cost—a payment to the factor capital in return for its contribution of risk-taking. But since we are no longer in a changeless circular flow economy, we can introduce a much more dynamic conception of profits. Now we can think of profits not merely as a factor cost (although there is always a certain element of risk-remuneration in profits), but as a return to especially efficient or forward-thinking firms who have used the investment process to introduce profitable new products or processes ahead of the run of their industries. We can think of profits, too, as being in part the return accruing to powerful firms who exact a semimonopolistic return from their customers.

What matters in our analysis is not the precise explanation we give to the origin of profits, but a precise explanation of their role in maintaining a "closed-circuit" economy in which all costs are returned to the marketplace as demand. A commonly heard diagnosis for economic maladies is that profits are at the root of the matter, in that they cause a "withdrawal" of spending power or income from the community. If profits were "hoarded," or kept unspent, this might be true. In fact, however, profits can be spent in three ways:

1. They may be distributed as income to the household sector as dividends or profit shares, to become part of household spending.

2. They may be spent by business firms for new plant and equipment.

3. They may be taxed by the government and spent in the public sector.

All three methods of offsetting profits appear in Fig. 4-7, on the next page.

We can see that profits need not constitute a withdrawal from the income stream. Indeed, unless profits are adequate, businesses will very likely not invest enough to offset the savings of the household sector. They may, in fact, even fail to make normal replacement expenditures, aggravating the demand gap still further in this way.

Thus the existence of profits, far from being deflationary— that is, far from causing a fall in income—is, in fact, essential for the maintenance of a given level of income or for an advance to a higher level. Nonetheless, there is a germ of truth in the contentions of those who have maintained that profits can cause an

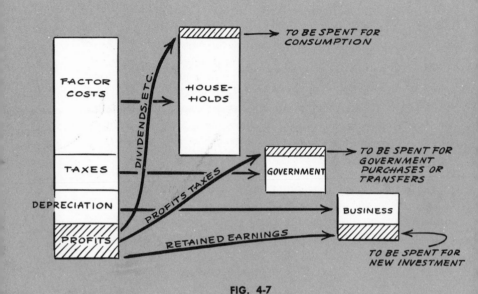

FIG. 4-7

insufficiency of purchasing power. For unless profits are returned to the flow of purchasing power as dividends that are *spent* by their recipients, or as new capital *expenditures* made by business, or as taxes that lead to additional public *spending*, there *will* be a gap in the community's demand. Thus we can think of profits just as we think of saving—an indispensable source of economic growth or a potential source of economic decline.

### Saving, Investment, and Growth

We are almost ready to leave our analysis of the circle of production and income, and to proceed to a much closer study of the individual dynamic elements that create and close gaps. Before we do, however, it is well that we take note of one last fact of the greatest importance. In offsetting the savings of any sector by investment, we have closed the production and income circuit, much as in the stationary circular flow, but there is one crucial difference from the circular flow. Now we have closed the flow by diverting savings into the creation of *additional* capital. Unlike the stationary circular flow where the handing around of incomes did no more than to maintain unchanged the original configuration of the system, in our new dynamic saving-and-investing model *each closing of the circuit results in a quantitative change—the addition of a new "layer" of capital.* Hence, more and more wealth is being added to our system; and thinking back to our first impressions of the interaction of wealth and population, we would expect more and more productiveness from our human factors. Bringing with it complications with which we shall have to deal in due course, *growth* has entered our economic model.

# 5

# The Consumption Sector

With a basic understanding of the crucial role of expenditure and of the complex relationship of saving and investment behind us, we are in a position to look more deeply into the question of the determination of gross national product. For what we have discovered heretofore is only the *mechanism* by which a market economy can sustain—or fail to sustain—a given level of output through a circuit of expenditure and receipt. Now we must try to discover the *forces* that dynamize the system, creating or closing gaps between income and outgo. Hence, beginning with this chapter, we devote our attention to the actual behavior of the household, government, and business sectors and to their respective motivations for consumption, government purchases, and investment.

## The Household Sector

Largest, most familiar, and in many respects most important of all the sectors in the economy is that of the nation's households—that is, its families and single-dwelling individuals (the two categories together called consumer units) considered as receivers of income and transfer payments, or as savers and spenders of money for consumption.

How big is this sector? In 1963 it comprised over forty-seven million families and eleven million independent individuals who collectively gathered in $464 billions and who spent $375 billions. As Fig. 5-1 shows, the great bulk of receipts was from factor earn-

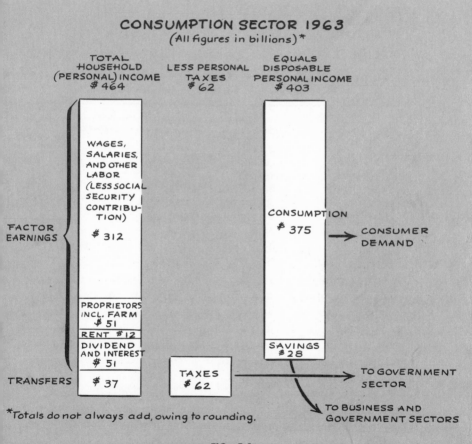

CONSUMPTION SECTOR 1963
*(All figures in billions)**

| TOTAL HOUSEHOLD (PERSONAL) INCOME $464 | LESS PERSONAL TAXES $62 | EQUALS DISPOSABLE PERSONAL INCOME $403 |

FACTOR EARNINGS

WAGES, SALARIES, AND OTHER LABOR (LESS SOCIAL SECURITY CONTRIBUTION) $312

CONSUMPTION $375 → CONSUMER DEMAND

PROPRIETORS INCL. FARM $51
RENT $12
DIVIDEND AND INTEREST $51

TRANSFERS $37

TAXES $62

SAVINGS $28

TAXES $62 → TO GOVERNMENT SECTOR

→ TO BUSINESS AND GOVERNMENT SECTORS

*Totals do not always add, owing to rounding.

**FIG. 5-1**

ings, and transfer payments played only a relatively small role. As we can also see, we must subtract personal tax payments from household income (or *personal income,* as it is officially designated) before we get *disposable personal income*—income actually available for spending. It is from disposable personal income that the crucial choice is made, to spend or save. Much of this chapter will focus on that choice.

## Consumption in Historic Perspective

Before we look into the patterns that lie behind this diagram it is well that we set the household sector in some general perspective vis-à-vis the rest of the economy. Table 5-1 relates

Table 5-1    GNP AND CONSUMPTION, SELECTED YEARS
(In billions of dollars at current prices)

| Year | GNP | Consumption | Consumption as % of GNP |
|------|------|------|------|
| 1929 | 104.4 | 79.0 | 76 |
| 1933 | 56.0 | 46.4 | 83 |
| 1940 | 100.6 | 71.9 | 71 |
| 1944 | 211.4 | 109.8 | 52 |
| 1960 | 502.6 | 328.2 | 65 |
| 1961 | 518.7 | 337.3 | 65 |
| 1962 | 556.2 | 356.8 | 64 |
| 1963 | 583.9 | 375.0 | 64 |

consumer buying to GNP for a number of crucial years: 1929, the last year of predepression prosperity; 1933, a year of deep depression; 1940, the last year of the prewar economy; 1944, a peak war year; and the individual years of the 1960's.*

Certain things stand out from this table that warrant our emphasis before we move into a closer examination of the dynamics of consumption.

1. *Consumption spending is by far the largest category of spending in GNP.* Total consumer expenditures—for durable goods, such as automobiles or washing machines; nondurables,

* In Appendix I, the reader will find a table of basic statistics for all years from 1929 through 1963. For sources of tables, see footnote to Table 2-1, p. 6.

like food or clothing; and services, such as recreation or medical care—account for approximately two-thirds of all the final buying in the economy.

2. *Consumption is not only the biggest, it is also the steadiest, of all the streams of expenditure.* For consumption, as we have mentioned, is the essential economic activity. Unless there is a total breakdown in the social system, households will consume some bare minimum. Further, it is a fact of common experience that even in adverse circumstances, households seek to maintain their accustomed living standards. Thus consumption activities constitute a kind of floor for the level of over-all economic activity. Investment and government spending, as we shall see, are capable of sudden reversals; but the streams of consumer spending tend to display a measure of stability over time.

3. *Consumption is nonetheless capable of considerable fluctuation as a proportion of GNP.* Remembering our previous diagrams, we can see that this proportionate fluctuation must reflect changes in the relative importance of investment and government spending. And indeed this is the case. As investment spending fell in the depression, consumption bulked relatively larger in GNP; as government spending increased during the war, consumption bulked relatively smaller. The changing *relative* size of consumption, in other words, reflects broad changes in *other* sectors rather than sharp changes in consuming habits.

4. *Despite its importance, consumption alone will not "buy back" GNP.* It is well to recall that consumption, although the largest component of GNP, is still *only* two-thirds of GNP. Government buying and business buying of investment goods are essential if the income–expenditure circuit is to be closed. During our subsequent analysis it will help to remember that consumption expenditure by itself does not provide the only impetus of demand.

## Saving in Historic Perspective

This first view of consumption activity sets the stage for our inquiry into the dynamic causes of fluctuations in GNP. We already know that the saving–investment relationship lies at the center of this problem, and that much saving arises from the household sector. Hence, let us see what we can learn about the saving process in historic perspective.

We begin with a table that shows us the relationship of household saving to disposable income—that is, to household sector incomes after the payment of taxes. Again we use the bench-mark years that will be our constant points of reference during our study.

Table 5-2    HISTORICAL RELATIONSHIPS OF SAVINGS AND INCOME

| Year | Disposable income | Savings | Savings as per cent of disposable income |
|------|-------------------|---------|------------------------------------------|
|      | (Billions of current dollars) | | |
| 1929 | 83.1 | 4.2 | 5.0 |
| 1933 | 45.7 | —0.7 | —1.5 |
| 1940 | 76.1 | 4.2 | 5.5 |
| 1944 | 146.8 | 36.9 | 25.1 |
| 1960 | 349.9 | 21.7 | 6.2 |
| 1961 | 364.7 | 27.3 | 7.5 |
| 1962 | 384.6 | 27.8 | 7.2 |
| 1963 | 402.5 | 27.5 | 6.8 |

What we see here are two interesting facts. First, during the bottom of the Great Depression there were *no* savings in the household sector. In fact, under the duress of unemployment, millions of households were forced to *dissave*—to borrow or to draw on their old savings (hence the negative figure for the sector as a whole). By way of contrast, we notice the immense savings of the peak war years when consumers' goods were scarce and households were exhorted to save. Clearly, then, the amount of saving is capable of great fluctuation, falling to zero or to negative figures in periods of great economic distress and rising to as much as a quarter of income during periods of goods shortages.

Second, however, we must be struck by another fact. However variable the amounts, the savings *ratio* shows an extraordinary stability in "normal" years. This steadiness is particularly noteworthy in postwar years. From 1950 to the present, as Fig. 5-2 shows, despite dips and trembles in the line, the ratio of

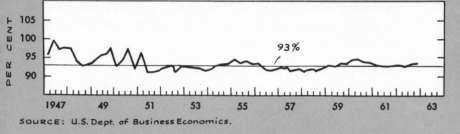

RATIO OF PERSONAL CONSUMPTION EXPENDITURES TO DISPOSABLE PERSONAL INCOME
Expenditures have averaged about 93% of income since 1950.

SOURCE: U.S. Dept. of Business Economics.

**FIG. 5-2**

consumption to disposable income has shown a marked stability, averaging 93 per cent of income, with annual deviations rarely in excess of 1 per cent.

### Long-Run Savings Behavior

This stability of the long-run savings ratio is an interesting and important phenomenon, and something of a puzzling one, for we might easily imagine that the savings ratio would rise over time. Statistical investigations of cross sections of the nation show that rich families tend to save not only larger amounts, but larger *percentages* of their income, than poor families do. Thus as the entire nation has grown richer, and as families have moved from lower income brackets to higher ones, it would seem natural to suppose that they would also take on the higher savings characteristics that accompany upper incomes.

Were this so, the economy would face a very serious problem. In order to sustain its higher levels of aggregate income, it would then have to invest an ever larger proportion of its income to offset its growing ratio of savings to income. As we shall see in our next chapter, investment is always a source of potential trouble because it is so much riskier than any other business function. If we had to keep on making proportionally larger investments each year to keep pace with our proportionally growing savings, we should live in an exceedingly vulnerable economic environment.

Fortunately, we are rescued from this dangerous situation, because our long-run savings ratio, as we have seen, displays a reassuring steadiness. In fact, there has been no significant upward trend in the savings ratio for the nation's households since the mid-1800's.

### Short- vs. Long-Run Savings Behavior

How do we reconcile this long-run stability with the fact that statistical studies always reveal that rich families *do* save a larger percentage of their incomes than poor families? As the nation has moved, en masse, into higher income brackets, why has it not also saved proportionately more of its income?

The answer hinges on important differences between the savings behavior of typical families over a short period of time and over a longer period. In the short run, families in every income bracket do indeed increase their savings sharply as their incomes rise. Much of a salary raise or a windfall is likely to be used *at first* for savings purposes. Debts may be quickly paid off. Money may be allowed to pile up in the bank while plans are made to readjust living standards. Even when the increase in income is used for a splurge such as the purchase of a new car, income may be allowed to lie idle for a short period. Thus, in the short run, savings ratios for additions to income are typically higher than they were before the increase was received.

What is true for the short run, however, is not true for the long run. From decade to decade, and even from year to year, powerful pressures and pervasive changes in our environment seem to operate on families at all levels, giving rise to a slow, secular decline in the desire to save. The growth of Social Security and pension plans, the impingement of higher income taxes, the steady expansion of advertising and consumer credit, the temptations of affluence, and the spirit of keeping up with the Joneses—all these influences appear to have worked a gradual decline in the long-run savings desires of *all* income groups. In addition, despite the statistics that show a steady rise in savings-ratios from income class to income class, it is likely that families in different income groups save much more nearly equal proportions of their incomes than our "cross section" data show.*

As a result of these and still other motivations, savings behavior in the long run differs considerably from that in the short run. Over the years, American households have shown a remarkable stability in their rate of over-all savings. Its importance has already been mentioned. In a shorter period of time, however—over a few months or perhaps a year—households tend to save higher fractions of increases in their incomes than they do in the long run. The very great importance of this fact we shall subsequently note.

## *The Consumption-Income Relationship*

What we have heretofore seen are some of the historical and empirical relationships of consumption and personal saving to income. We have taken the trouble to investigate these relationships in some detail, since they are among the most important causes of the gaps that have to be closed by investment. But the statistical facts in themselves are only a halfway stage in our macroeconomic investigation. Now we want to go beyond the facts to a generalized understanding of what they mean. Thus our next task is to extract from the facts certain *relationships* that are sufficiently regular and dependable for us to build into a new dynamic model of the economy.

If we reflect back over the data we have examined, one primary conclusion comes to mind. This is the indisputable fact

* For instance, middle-class families who have suffered temporary reverses (and who are therefore counted in lower than their "regular" income brackets) will typically maintain their living standards and reduce their savings, thereby causing a lower savings ratio for these lower brackets than would be found if we included only "permanent" members of it. Conversely, families that have had a lucky year and are temporary residents of a higher bracket may save more than is customary for regular residents of that bracket, thereby exaggerating the saving propensities of the upper groups. The motivation to save, in order to provide future well-being, may well result in surprisingly similar savings ratios, at least in the broad spectrum of income brackets between the very low and the very high.

that the *amount* of saving generated by the household sector depends in the first instance upon the income enjoyed by the household sector. To be sure, the *ratio* of saving will vary in the short run from the longer "settled" run. But of the primary dependence of the *amount* of saving on the level of income, there can be no doubt.

## The Propensity to Consume Schedule

We call this basic relationship the *propensity to consume,* giving it the name invented by the brilliant English economist John Maynard Keynes,* the first economist to place the income–consumption relationship at the center of macroeconomic analysis.

Exactly what do we mean by the propensity to consume? We mean that the relationship between consumption and income is sufficiently dependable so that we can draw a "schedule" showing how much consumption (and therefore, of course, how much saving) will be associated with various levels of income. Such a schedule—a purely hypothetical one—might be represented by Table 5-3.

Table 5-3　　SCHEDULE OF THE PROPENSITY TO CONSUME
(In billions of dollars)

| Income | Consumption | Savings |
|--------|-------------|---------|
| 100 | 80 | 20 |
| 110 | 87 | 23 |
| 120 | 92 | 28 |
| 130 | 95 | 35 |
| 140 | 97 | 43 |

One could imagine, of course, innumerable different propensity to consume schedules; in one society a given income might be accompanied by a much higher ratio of saving than in another. But the basic hypothesis of Keynes—a hypothesis amply confirmed by research—was that the propensity to consume

* The name, incidentally, is pronounced "Kanes," not "Keenes."

schedule in all modern industrial societies had a particular basic configuration, despite these variations. The propensity to consume, said Keynes, reflected the fact that on the average, *men tended to increase their consumption as their incomes rose, but not by as much as their income.* In other words, as the incomes of individuals rose, so did both their consumption *and their savings.*

Note that Keynes did not say that the proportion of saving rose. We have seen how involved is the dynamic determination of savings ratios. Keynes merely suggested that the *amount* of saving would rise as income rose—or to put it conversely again, that families would not use *all* their increases in income for consumption purposes alone. It is well to remember that these conclusions hold in going down the schedule as well as up. Keynes' basic "law" implies that when there is a decrease in income, there will be some decrease in the *amount of saving,* or that a family will not absorb a fall in its income entirely by contracting its consumption.

What does the propensity to consume schedule look like in the United States? We will come to that shortly. First, however, let us fill in our understanding of the terms we will need for our generalized study.

## The Average and Marginal Propensity to Consume

The propensity to consume schedule gives us two ways of measuring the fundamental economic relationship of income and saving. One way is simply to take any given level of income and to compute the percentage relation of consumption to that income. This gives us the *average propensity to consume.* In Table 5-4, using the same hypothetical schedule as before, we make this computation.

The average propensity to consume, in other words, tells us how a society at any given moment divides its total income between consumption and saving. It is thus a kind of measure of long-run savings behavior, for the ratios in which households divide their income between saving and consuming reflect established habits and, as we have seen, do not ordinarily change rapidly.

Table 5-4   CALCULATION OF THE AVERAGE PROPENSITY TO CONSUME

| Income | Consumption | Consumption divided by income (Average propensity |
|---|---|---|
| | (Billions of dollars) | to consume) |
| 100 | 80 | .80 |
| 110 | 87 | .79 |
| 120 | 92 | .77 |
| 130 | 95 | .73 |
| 140 | 97 | .69 |

But we can also use our schedule to measure another very important aspect of saving behavior: the way households divide *increases* (or decreases) in income between consumption and saving. This *marginal propensity to consume* is quite different from the average propensity to consume, as the figures in Table 5-5 (still from our original hypothetical schedule) demonstrate.

Table 5-5   CALCULATION OF THE MARGINAL PROPENSITY TO CONSUME

| Income | Consumption | Change in income | Change in consumption | (Marginal propensity to consume) = Change in consumption divided by change in income |
|---|---|---|---|---|
| | (Billions of dollars) | | | |
| 100 | 80 | — | — | — |
| 110 | 87 | 10 | 7 | .70 |
| 120 | 92 | 10 | 5 | .50 |
| 130 | 95 | 10 | 3 | .30 |
| 140 | 97 | 10 | 2 | .20 |

Much of economics, in micro- as well as macroanalysis, is concerned with studying the effects of *changes* in economic life. It is precisely here that marginal concepts take on their importance. When we speak of the average propensity to consume, we relate all consumption and all income from the bottom up, so to speak, and thus we call attention to behavior covering a great variety of situations and conditions. But when we speak of the marginal propensity to consume, we are focusing only on our behavior in regard to our *changed* incomes. Thus the marginal approach is invaluable, as we shall see, in dealing with the effects of short-run fluctuations in GNP.

## A Diagram of the Propensity to Consume

The essentially simple idea of a systematic relationship between income and consumption will play an extremely important part in the model of the economy we shall soon construct. But the relationships we have thus far defined are too vague to be of much usefulness. We want to know if we can extract from the facts of experience not only a general dependence of consumption on income, but a *fairly precise method of determining exactly how much saving will be associated with a given amount of income.*

Here we reach a place where it will help us to use diagrams and simple equations rather than words alone. So let us begin by transferring our conception of a propensity to consume schedule to a new kind of diagram directly showing the interrelation of income and consumption.

The *scatter diagram* on p. 72 shows precisely that. Along the vertical axis on the left we have marked off intervals to measure total consumer expenditure in billions of dollars; along the horizontal axis on the bottom we measure disposable personal income, also in billions of dollars. The dots tell us, for the year that the numerals indicate, how large consumption and income were. For instance, if we take the topmost dot (for 1963) and look directly below it to the horizontal axis, we can see that disposable personal income for that year was roughly $400 billions. The same dot measured against the vertical consumption axis tells us that consumption for 1963 was approximately $375 billions.

If we consult a table, we will find the actual values: $402.5 billions for disposable income, and $375.0 for consumption. Further, if we now divide the figure for consumption by that for income, we get a value of 93.2 per cent for our propensity to consume. If we subtract that from 100, our propensity to save must have been 6.8 per cent, the same figure, of course, as in Table 5-2, on p. 64.

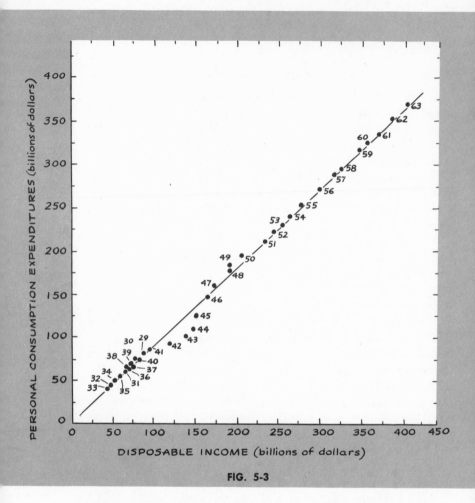

**FIG. 5-3**

Notice that the black line which "fits" the trend of the dots does not go evenly from corner to corner. If it did, it would mean that each amount of income was matched by an *equal* amount of consumption—in other words, that there was no saving. Instead, the line leans slightly downward, indicating that as income goes higher, consumption also increases, but not by quite as much.

If we now measure the *angle* of the "trend line" that fits any particular year (and this line will be ever so slightly different as we alter our terminal years), we have our average propensity to consume for that year.

Does the chart also show us our marginal propensity to consume? Indeed it does. If you take any single year and look at the changes in consumption and income from that year to the next, you will be considering the marginal propensity to consume. Note that for many years, especially in the 1950's and 1960's, the marginal propensity to consume (if we drew it as a line connecting each pair of dots) would virtually coincide with the average propensity to consume.

Not so, however, for all years, as an inspection of the chart will show. During the war years, for instance, as the result of a shortage of many consumer goods and a general exhortation to save, the marginal propensity to consume was unusually low. That is why the dots during those years form a bulge below the main trend line. After the war, we can also see that increases in income resulted in very high proportional increases in consumption. As a matter of fact, for a few years consumption actually rose *faster* than income, as people drew down their wartime savings to make up for wartime shortages. By 1950, however, the consumption–income relationship was back to virtually the same ratio as during the 1930's.

## The Propensity to Consume, in Simple Mathematics

There is another way of reducing to shorthand clarity the propensity to consume idea, at least for those who find simple mathematics an expressive language. Even those who do not should try to follow the very simple formulas presented, if only because we shall often use the letters as abbreviations in our subsequent chapters.

We begin by giving letters to the words we use again and again.

$$C = \text{consumption}$$
$$I = \text{investment}$$

$$S = \text{saving}$$
$$Y = \text{income}$$

Finally, we use the symbol $f\ (\quad)$ to express the idea of relationship. Read it "function of (whatever is included in the parentheses)."

Now when we talk of $C = f(Y)$, we read it aloud as "consumption is a function of income." What this means is that consumption is related to income in some manner that can be described by a mathematical relationship.

What kind of relationship? Highly sophisticated and complex formulas have been tried to "fit" the values of $C$ and $Y$, their economics and their mathematics both beyond the scope of this book. But we can at least get a clearer idea of what it means to devise a *consumption function* by trying to make a very simple one ourselves. If we look at Fig. 5-3 on p. 72, we can see that during the Depression years, at very low levels of income, around $50 billion, consumption was just as large as income itself. (In some years it was actually bigger; as we have seen, there was net dissaving in 1933.) Hence, we might hypothesize that a consumption function for the United States might have a fixed value representing this "bottom," and some regular fraction designating the amount of income that would be saved for all income over that amount. Furthermore, recalling the stability of the savings ratio of 7 per cent (at least in postwar years) we might hypothesize that we will consume 93 per cent of all income over the "bottom."

In point of fact, such a formula would yield roughly accurate results. For 1963, for instance, it would predict that total consumption would equal $50 billions plus 93 per cent of all income over $50 billions. This gives us a figure of $378 billions for consumption in 1963—not very far from the actual figure of $375 billions. Let the reader be warned, however, that devising a consumption function is much more difficult than this simple and uncritical test would indicate. Nonetheless, it gives one an idea of what the economist hopes to find—a precise way of expressing the relationship between $C$ and $Y$, which can then be used for *predicting* changes in $C$ in the future.*

## The Passivity of Consumption

Throughout this chapter we have talked of the dynamics of consuming and saving. Now it is important that we recall the main conclusion of our analysis, *the essential passivity of consumption as an economic process.* Consumption spending, we will recall, is a function of income. This means it is a *dependent* variable in the economic process, a factor that is acted *on,* but that does not itself generate spontaneous action.

To be sure, it is well to qualify this assertion. We have earlier paid special attention to the long-term stability of the savings ratio and pointed out that one cause of this stability was a general movement of all households toward consumption as their incomes grew. This dynamic, although slow-acting, behavioral trend has exerted a strong background force on the trend of the economy. Then, too, there have been occasions, the most famous being the years just following World War II, when consumption seemed to generate its own momentum and raced out ahead of income. But this was a period when wants were intense, following wartime shortages, and when huge amounts of wartime savings were available to translate those wants into action. During the normal course of things, however, no matter how intense wants may be, consumers ordinarily lack the spend-

---

* For those who are at home in simple algebra, we can generalize our results. We begin with a simple hypothetical formulation of the consumption function as follows:

$C = Y_0 + c(Y - Y_0)$, where
$C$ = consumption
$Y_0$ = the value of disposable income at the "bottom" (where $Y = C$)
$c$ = long-run ratio of $C$ to $Y$, and
$Y$ = current value of disposable income.

Substituting values for the United States in 1963, we get

$Y_0$ = \$50 billions
$c$ = .93
$Y$ = \$403. Thus,
$C$ = \$50 + .93(\$403 − \$50) = \$378 billions.

able cash to make them part of the effective demand of the economy.

It is important to remember that wants and appetites *alone* do not drive the economy upward; if they did, we should experience a more impelling demand in depressions, when people are hungry, than in booms, when they are well off. Hence the futility of those who urge the cure of depressions by suggesting that consumers should buy more! There is nothing that most consumers would rather do than buy more, if only they could. Let us not forget, furthermore, that consumers are at all times being cajoled and exhorted to increase their expenditures by the multibillion dollar pressures exerted by the advertising industry.

*The trouble is, however, that consumers cannot buy more unless they have more incomes to buy with.* It is true, of course, that for short periods they can borrow or they may temporarily sharply reduce their rate of savings; but each household's borrowing capacity or accumulated savings are limited, so that once these bursts are over, the steady habitual ways of saving and spending reassert themselves.

Thus it is clear that in considering the consumer sector we study a part of the economy that, however ultimately important, is not in itself the source of major changes in activity. Consumption mirrors and, as we shall see, can magnify disturbances elsewhere in the economy, but it does not initiate the greater part of our economic fortunes or misfortunes. For that, we must turn to the two remaining great sectors, where we shall find the driving elements of our economic mechanism.

# 6

# *The Investment Sector*

Consumption is an activity everyone knows as an experienced economic actor in his own right; investing, on the other hand, is an economy activity foreign to most of us. For investing, in the context of macroeconomic analysis, has very little to do with the kind of "investing" familiar to us in the selection of stocks or bonds as personal assets. Investing, as the economist sees it, is an activity that uses the resources of the community to maintain or add to its stock of capital wealth.

Now this may or may not coincide with the purchase of a security. When we buy an ordinary stock or bond, we usually buy it from someone who has previously owned it, and therefore our personal act of "investment" becomes, in the economic view of things, merely a *transfer* of claims without any direct bearing on the creation of new wealth. A pays B cash and takes his General Manufacturing stock; B takes A's cash and doubtless uses it to buy stock from C; but the transactions between A and B and C in no way alter the actual amount of real capital in the economy. Only when we buy *newly issued* shares or bonds, and then only when their proceeds are directly allocated to new equipment or plant, does our act of personal financial investment result in the

77

addition to wealth to the community. In that case, A buys his stock directly (or through an investment banker) from General Manufacturing itself, and not from B. A's cash can now be spent for new capital goods, as presumably it will be.

Thus investment, as the economist sees it, is a relatively little-known form of activity for the great majority of us. This is true not only because real investment is not the same as personal financial investment, but because the real investors of the nation usually act on behalf of an institution other than the familiar one of the household. The unit of behavior in the world of investment is typically the business *firm*, just as in the world of consumption it is the household. Boards of directors, chief executives, or small businesses proprietors are the persons who decide whether or not to devote business cash to the construction of new facilities or to the addition of inventory; and this decision, as we shall see, is very different in character and motivation from the decisions familiar to us as members of the household sector.

## *Main Attributes*

Before we begin an investigation into the dynamics of investment decisions, however, let us gain a quick acquaintance with the sector as a whole, much as we did with the consumption sector.

The diagram opposite gives a first general impression of the investment sector in a recent year. Note that the main source of gross private domestic investment expenditure comes from retained earnings of corporations, that is, from profits that have not been distributed as dividends or paid to the government as taxes. However, as the next bar shows, gross investment *expenditures* are considerably larger than retained earnings. The difference represents funds that business obtains in several ways.

1. It may draw on cash (or securities) accumulated out of retained earnings of *previous* years.

2. It may obtain savings from the household sector by direct borrowing, or by sale of new issues of shares of stock, or indirectly via insurance companies, or savings banks, or pension funds, etc.

3. It may borrow from commercial banks.

## BUSINESS SECTOR, 1962
(All figures in billions)*

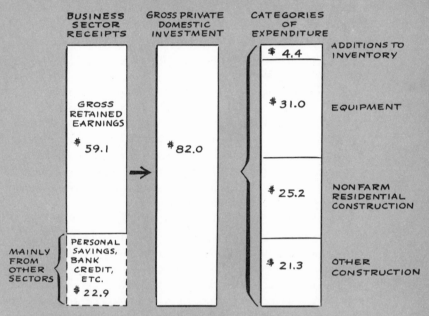

| BUSINESS SECTOR RECEIPTS | GROSS PRIVATE DOMESTIC INVESTMENT | CATEGORIES OF EXPENDITURE |
|---|---|---|

GROSS RETAINED EARNINGS $ 59.1

$ 82.0

$ 4.4 ADDITIONS TO INVENTORY

$ 31.0 EQUIPMENT

$ 25.2 NON FARM RESIDENTIAL CONSTRUCTION

MAINLY FROM OTHER SECTORS

PERSONAL SAVINGS, BANK CREDIT, ETC. $ 22.9

$ 21.3 OTHER CONSTRUCTION

* Figures do not always add, owing to rounding.

**FIG. 6-1**

The last of these sources of funds we will not fully understand until we reach Chapter 9, when we study the money mechanism. But it is already easy to see that the bulk of investment expenditures are financed by business itself from its retained earnings. The plowing back of profits and the reinvestment of depreciation accruals thus constitute the main sources of capital formation. We might also note that the stock markets, although indispensable for personal financial investment, play only a minor role in financing real investment. In 1961, a year that saw large new issues, the total amount of net new capital raised on the stock markets was less than $3 billion.

## The Categories of Investment

1. *Inventories.* From the total funds at its disposal, the business sector now renews its worn-out capital and adds new capital. Let us say a word concerning some of the main categories of investment expenditure.

At the top of our diagrammatic bar we note an item of $4.4 billions for *additions to inventory.* Note that this figure does not represent total inventories, but only *changes* in inventories, upwards or downwards. If there had been no change in inventory over the year, the item would have been zero, even if existing inventories were huge. Why? Because those huge inventories would have been included in the investment expenditure flow of *previous* years when they were built up.

Additions to inventories are capital, but they need not be additions to capital *goods.* Indeed, they are likely to include farm stocks, consumers goods, and other items of all kinds. Of course, these are goods held by business, and not by consumers. But that is the very point. We count inventory additions as net investment because they are output that has been produced but that has not been consumed. In another year, if these goods pass from the hands of business into consumers' hands, and inventories decline, we will have a negative figure for net inventory investment. This will mean, just as it appears, that we are consuming goods faster than we are producing them—that we are disinvesting.

Investments in inventory are particularly significant for one reason. Alone among the investment categories, inventories can be *rapidly* used up as well as increased. A positive figure for one year or even one calendar quarter can quickly turn into a negative figure the next. *This means that expenditures for inventory are usually the most volatile element of any in gross national product.* As we shall see, in the accumulation or decumulation

of inventory lies a powerful lever for general economic acceleration or deceleration.

2. *Equipment.* The next item in our bar is more familiar:
$31 billions for *equipment*. Here we find expenditures for goods
of a varied sort—lathes, trucks, generators, computers, office type-
writers. The total includes both new equipment and replacement
equipment, and we need a word of caution here. Exactly what
does it mean to "replace" a given item of equipment? Suppose
we have a textile loom that cost $100,000 and that is now on its
last legs. Is the loom "replaced" by spending another $100,000,
regardless of what kind of machine the money will buy? Suppose
loom prices have gone up and $100,000 no longer buys a loom of
the same capacity? Or suppose that prices have remained steady;
but that owing to technological advance, $100,000 now buys a
loom of double the old capacity. Such questions make the definition of "replacement" an accountant's headache and an economist's nightmare. We need not involve ourselves deeper in the
question, but we should note the complexities introduced into a
seemingly simple question once we leave the changeless world of
a stationary flow and enter the world of invention and innovation.

3. *Construction.* Our next section on the diagrammatic bar
is nonfarm *residential construction*. Why do we include this item
of $25.2 billions in the investment sector when most of it is repre-
sented by new houses that householders buy for their own use?

The answer is that most houses are built by business firms
(such as contractors and developers) who put up the houses *before*
they are sold. Thus the original expenditures involved in building houses typically come from businessmen, not from households. Later, when the householder buys a house, he takes possession of an *existing* asset, and his expenditure does not pump
new incomes out into the economy, but only repays the contractor
who *did* pump new incomes out.

The last item on the bar, $21.3 billion of other *construction*,
is largely made up of the "plant" in "plant and equipment"—
factories and stores and private office buildings and warehouses.
It does not, however, include public construction such as roads,

dams, harbors, or public buildings, all of which are picked up under government purchases. It is interesting to note that the building of structures, as represented by the total of residential construction plus other private construction, accounts for over half of all investment expenditure, and this total would be further swelled if public construction were included herein. This accords with the dominant role of structures in the panorama of national wealth we first encountered in Chapter 1. It tells us, too, that swings in construction expenditure can be a major lever for economic change.

## Investment in Historic Perspective

With this introduction behind us, let us take a look at the flow of investment, not over a single year, but in perspective, over many years. In Table 6-1, we can trace the course of invest-

Table 6-1    GROSS PRIVATE DOMESTIC INVESTMENT
(In billions of current dollars)

| Year | GNP | Gross private domestic investment | Gross investment as per cent of GNP |
|------|------|------|------|
| 1929 | 104.4 | 16.2 | 15.5 |
| 1933 | 56.0 | 1.4 | 2.5 |
| 1940 | 100.6 | 13.2 | 13.1 |
| 1944 | 211.4 | 7.1 | 3.4 |
| 1960 | 502.6 | 71.8 | 14.3 |
| 1961 | 518.7 | 68.8 | 13.3 |
| 1962 | 556.2 | 79.1 | 14.2 |
| 1963 | 583.9 | 82.0 | 14.0 |

ment over the same indicative years that we used in the case of consumption.

Several things spring to our notice. First, we see that gross investment in the depths of the depression virtually disappeared, that we almost failed to *maintain,* much less add to, our stock of wealth. (Net investment was, in fact, a negative figure for several years.)

Next we note that private investment during the war peak

year was pushed aside (by means of strict allocations that made it impossible for businessmen to obtain materials) in order to make way for war production. And finally, we note that investment in recent years, although very large in absolute figures, in percentage terms is not quite back to the 1929 relation to GNP.

## The Instability of Investment

There is an impression that follows from this. It is the extreme *instability of investment*. Unlike the passive flow of consumption expenditure, we do not find investment tagging along with great regularity as income changes. Rather, it is typical of investment that it takes sudden, violent changes in course *ahead of, or in the opposite direction to, income*.

Furthermore, where consumption spending is cushioned by the behavior patterns summed up on Keynes' formulation of the propensity to consume, investment expenditure has no such restraining motivation in the background; we can construct no neat schedules relating $I$ to $Y$ similar to the relation of $C$ to $Y$.

Thus investment is capable of much more drastic changes than is consumption. From 1929 to 1933, for example, while consumption fell by 41 per cent (see Table 5-1 on p. 62), investment fell by 92 per cent, as we can see on Table 6-1. (If we use figures that are corrected for price changes, consumption in "real terms" declined only by 20 per cent while real investment still fell off by about 80 per cent.) Similarly, while consumption rose by a little more than half from 1933 to 1940, investment in the same period rose nearly ninefold.

## The Importance of Investment

The instability of investment offers one reason why gross national product itself shows signs of instability. There is often a tendency among noneconomists to equate all buying in the economy with consumer buying. Let us never lose sight of the fact that the maintenance of, and addition to, capital is also a part of GNP spending and that a considerable part of the labor force depends for its livelihood on the making of investment goods. Indeed, at the bottom of the Great Depression in 1933, it was estimated that one-third of total unemployment was directly associated with the shrinkage in the capital goods industry.

We shall want to look more closely into the reasons for the extreme sensitivity of investment spending. But first a question must surely have occurred to the reader. For all its susceptibility to change, the investment sector is, after all, a fairly small sector. In 1963, total expenditures for gross private domestic investment came to only about 14 per cent of GNP, and the normal year-to-year variation in investment spending in the 1950's and 1960's was only about $5 billion to $10 billion, or 1 to 2 per cent of GNP. To devote so much time to such small fluctuations seems a disproportionate emphasis. How could so small a tail as investment wag so large a dog as GNP?

## The Multiplier

The answer lies in a relationship of economic activities known as the *multiplier*. The multiplier describes the fact that *additions to spending (or diminutions in spending) have an impact on income that is greater than the original increase or decrease in spending itself.* In other words, even small increments in spending can *multiply* their effects (whence the name).

It is not difficult to understand the general idea of the multiplier. Suppose that we have an island community whose economy is in a perfect circular flow, unchanging from year to year. Next, let us introduce the stimulus of a new investment expenditure in the form of a stranger who arrives from another island (with a supply of acceptable money) and who proceeds to build a house. This immediately increases the islanders' incomes. In our case, we will assume that our stranger spends $1,000 on wages for construction workers, and we will ignore all other expenditures he may make. (We also make the assumption that these workers were previously unemployed, so that our stranger is not merely taking them from some other task.)

Now the construction workers, who have had their incomes increased by $1,000, are very unlikely to sit on this money. As we know from our study of the marginal propensity to consume, they are apt to save some of the increase (and they may have to pay some to the government as income taxes), but the rest they will spend on additional consumption goods. Let us suppose that they save 10 per cent and pay taxes of 20 per cent on the $1,000 they get. They will then have $700 left over to spend for additional consumer goods and services.

But this is not an end to it. The sellers of these goods and services will now have received $700 over and above their former incomes, and they, too, will be certain to spend a considerable amount of their new income. If we assume that their family spending patterns (and their tax brackets) are the same as the construction workers, they will also spend 70 per cent of their new incomes, or $490. And now the wheel takes another turn, as still *another* group receives new income and spends a fraction of it, in turn.

## The Continuing Impact of Respending

If our stranger now departed as mysteriously as he came, we would have to describe the economic impact of his investment as constituting a single "bulge" of income that gradually disappeared. The bulge would consist of the original $1,000, the secondary $700, the tertiary $490, and so on. If everyone continued to spend 70 per cent of his new income, after ten rounds all that would remain by way of new spending traceable to the original $1,000 would be about $38. Soon, the impact of the new investment on incomes would have virtually disappeared.

But now let us suppose that after our visitor builds his house and leaves, another visitor arrives to build another house. This time, in other words, we assume that the level of investment spending *continues* at the higher level to which it was raised by the first expenditure for a new house. We can see that the second house will set into motion precisely the same repercussive effects as did the first, and that the new series of respendings will be added to the dwindling echoes of the original injection of incomes.

In Fig. 6-2, we can trace this effect. The succession of white bars at the bottom of the graph stands for the continuing injections of $1,000 as new houses are steadily built. (Note that this means the level of new investment is only being maintained, not that it is rising.) Each of these white bars now generates a series

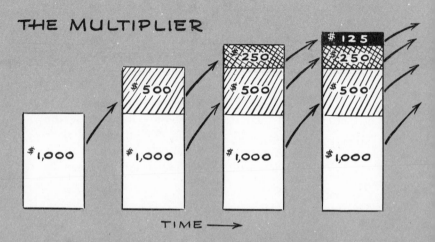

**THE MULTIPLIER**

TIME →

**FIG. 6-2**

of secondary, tertiary, etc., bars that represent the respending of income after taxes and savings. In our example we have assumed that the respending fraction is 50 per cent.

Our diagram shows us two very important things.

1. *A steady flow of new investment generates an equally steady but larger flow of total incomes.* It is very important to note that the incomes generated by respending are *just as permanent* as those due to the flow of investment itself.

2. We see, as well, that *the rise in income due to a continuing flow of new investment gradually levels out.* As the successive respending fractions become smaller, the rise in income approaches a plateau.

### The Marginal Propensity to Save

We can understand now that *the multiplier is the numerical relation between the initial new investment and the total increase in income.* If the initial investment is $1,000 and the total addition to income due to the respending of that $1,000 is $3,000, we have a multiplier of 3; if the total addition is $2,000, the multiplier is 2.

What determines how large the multiplier will be? The answer obviously depends in large measure on the spending and saving habits of income receivers with respect to additions to (or subtractions from) their incomes. The more they are inclined to save as incomes rise, the less will be available for respending, and the smaller will be the multiplier. Conversely, the less they save out of increases in income, the greater will be the multiplier.

We call the fraction of new income that is saved *the marginal propensity to save* (mps). Clearly, this fraction is the complement of a very familiar one, the marginal propensity to consume. If our marginal propensity to consume is 80 per cent, our marginal propensity to save must be 20 per cent; if our mpc is 70 per cent, our mps must be 30 per cent.

Understanding the relationship between the marginal propensity to save and the resulting size of the respending fractions allows us to state a very simple formula for the multiplier:

Change in income = multiplier × change in investment.

Using the symbol $\Delta$, delta, for the words "change in," and the fraction $\dfrac{1}{\text{mps}}$ for the word "multiplier," we have a formula that expresses the relationship we want:

$$\Delta Y = \frac{1}{\text{mps}} \times \Delta I$$

Suppose investment changes by \$10 billion and the mps is $\frac{1}{5}$, or 20 per cent. What will $\Delta Y$ be? Our formula tells us:

$$\Delta Y = \frac{1}{\frac{1}{5}} \times 10{,}000{,}000{,}000 \text{ or } \frac{1}{.20} \times 10{,}000{,}000{,}000$$

$$= 5 \times 10{,}000{,}000{,}000$$

$$= 50{,}000{,}000{,}000$$

This enables us to see that the *leverage on income exerted by new investment is governed by size of the marginal savings fraction.* If, e.g., mps were $\frac{1}{4}$, the change in income would be \$40 billion. If mps were 1—i.e., if the island construction workers saved all

---

* Note that mps is a *compound*, not simple, fraction. In the case above, mps is 1 *divided* by $\frac{1}{5}$. *It is not* $\frac{1}{5}$. Many mistakes in calculating the multiplier are made by students who forget this fact.

their new pay—then $\dfrac{1}{mps}$ would also be 1, and the impact of new investment on income no more than the $1,000 they earned initially.

## Leakages

The importance of marginal saving in giving to an increment of income a greater or lesser multiplicative impact is thus apparent. But as our example of the island economy has already shown us, savings are not the only "leakage" that lowers the impact of the multiplier. As incomes are passed from hand to hand, a substantial part of each round of receipts may also be channeled into tax avenues, or into retained earnings of business, or into buying goods from abroad. As with personal savings, these leakages *can* be respent by the business sector, by government, or by foreigners. But this respending depends on altogether independent decisions of business, government, or foreigners, and it is no longer the sheerly "automatic" effect of successive respending for consumption purposes.

All told, the sum of all these leakages—*personal savings, taxes, business savings,* and *imports*—very considerably reduces the multiplicative effect of a given increment of spending. Although the actual marginal propensity to save in the 1960's is about 7.5 per cent, the multiplier is nothing like the thirteen-fold impact we would expect.* Leakages reduce the estimated actual effect of an increment of spending on GNP to about 2 or a little more. The actual estimated leakages (except for imports) are shown in Fig. 6-3.

## The Multiplier and Investment

We have dwelt in some detail on the multiplier, for it answers the question of how changes in a relatively small sector, such as investment, can nonetheless bring about considerably larger total economic movements. If the actual multiplier effect of investment on GNP is 2, then a change of $5 billion to $10 billion in investment can bring about a total change in GNP of

* If the multiplier ratio $= \dfrac{1}{mps}$, then for the U.S., where mps = 7.5 per cent, we would expect the multiplier to equal 13.3.

## DISTRIBUTION OF AN ADDITIONAL DOLLAR OF GNP

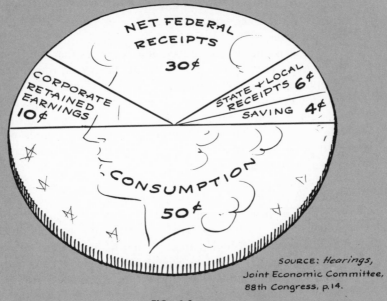

SOURCE: *Hearings,*
Joint Economic Committee,
88th Congress, p. 14.

FIG. 6-3

from $10 billion to $20 billion, by no means a negligible figure. In addition, as we shall shortly see, the multiplier may set up repercussions that feed back onto investment. But more of that momentarily. First let us make two last points in regard to the multiplier.

1. *Other multipliers.* We have talked of the multiplier in connection with changes in investment spending. But we must also realize that *any* change in any spending has a multiplier effect. An increase in foreigners' purchases of our exports has a multiplier effect, as does an increase in government spending or a decrease in taxes, or a spontaneous increase in consumption itself due to, say, a drop in the propensity to save. Any stimulus to the economy is thus not confined to its original impact, but gives a series of successive pushes to the system until it has been

absorbed into the normal circuit of expenditure and receipt. We shall come back to this important fact in our next chapter.

2. *Idle resources.* Finally, there is a very important proviso to recognize, although we will not study its full significance until Chapter 9. This is the important difference between an economy with idle resources—unemployed labor or unused machines or land—and one without them.

For it is only when we have idle resources that the responding impetus of the multiplier is useful. Then each round of new expenditure can now bring idle resources into use, creating not only new incomes but *new production and employment.* The situation is considerably different when there are no, or few, idle men or machines. Then the expenditure rounds of the multiplier bring higher money incomes, but these are not matched by the increased output.

In both cases, the multiplier exerts its leverage, bringing about an increase in total expenditure larger than the original injection of new spending. In the case without idle resources, however, the results are solely *inflationary,* as the increased spending results in higher incomes and higher prices, but not in higher output. In the case where idle resources exist, we can avoid this mere "money" multiplication and enjoy a rise in output as a result of our increased spending. Indeed, we can even speak of the *employment multiplier* in situations where there is considerable unemployment, meaning by this the total increase in employment brought about by a given increase in spending. We shall return in subsequent chapters to a fuller scrutiny of the difference between the case of idle and of fully employed resources, but we must bear the distinction in mind henceforth.

## The Downward Multiplier

The multiplier, with its extraordinary magnifying action, rests at the very center of our understanding of economic fluctuations. Not only does it explain how relatively small stimuli can exert considerable upward pushes, but it also makes much clearer than before how the failure to offset a small savings gap can snowball into a serious fall in income and employment.

For just as additional income is respent to create still further new income, a loss in income will not stop with the affected households, who might "patriotically" maintain their former rate of consumption spending by drawing on old savings or going into debt. On the contrary, as families lose income, they cut down on their spending, although the behavior pattern of the propensity to consume schedule suggests that they will not cut their consumption by as much as their loss in income. *Yet each reduction in consumption, small or large, lessens to that extent the income or receipts of some other household or firm.*

Thus we can speak of the downward effects of the multiplier, quite as much as the upward effects. If the multiplier in the U.S. is roughly 2, an initial fall in income, perhaps by a reduction in investment of $10 billion, will result in a total fall of income of $20 billion.

## The Multiplier and Economic Behavior

We have seen how crucial is the influence of the multiplier relationship in magnifying relatively small initial changes in expenditure into much larger ultimate changes in income. Now we must learn how to fit the idea of the multiplier relationship into our model of the economic system. But before we turn to that, a word of caution is in order.

Because we use the word *multiplier* so frequently in macro-economic analysis, it is easy to assume that the word refers to a basic aspect of economic behavior. It does not. The multiplier is only a *relationship*, not, in itself, an empirical fact of the real world. You cannot go out and directly find the multiplier the way you can go out and directly find levels of prices or flows of expenditure. Rather, to track down the multiplier, you must go in search of the underlying realities of economic behavior that give rise to the relationship itself.

What are those underlying realities? One of them is our be-havior in regard to spending and saving additions to (or sub-tractions from) our incomes. Another is the structure of taxes that channels part of income changes to the government. Still another reality is the market structure that permits some businesses to put away part of their receipts as profit (which is not likely to be automatically respent). These are the observable realities out of which the multiplier effect flows; and it is well that we keep in mind, as we continue to use the indispensable term, *multiplier,* that the word is only a shorthand reference to these real attributes of economic life.

# 7

# *Investment and Equilibrium*

We have spent some time investigating how variations in investment spending can induce powerful repercussions in the national economy. But we have not yet asked the all-important question of why the flow of capital expenditure should be variable in the first place. Nor have we understood how GNP will settle down after it has been raised or lowered by more or less investment. In this chapter, we must look into these matters—into the motives behind the investment expenditure of the firm, and into the way that changes in investment can shift GNP from one level to another.

## *The Motivation of Investment*

Consumption spending, let us remember, is essentially directed at the satisfaction of the person. In an increasingly affluent society, we may not be able to say that consumer expenditure is any longer geared to necessity, but at least it obeys the fairly constant promptings of the cultural and social environment, with the result that consumer spending, in the aggregate, fluctuates relatively little, except as income fluctuates.

A quite different set of motivations drives the investment impulse. Whether the investment is for replacement of old capi-

tal or for the installation of new capital, the ruling consideration is virtually never the personal use or satisfaction that the
investment yields to the owners of the firm. Instead the touch-
stone of investment decisions is the *profit* investments are expected to yield in future production.

Note the important stress on *expectations*. One firm may be
enjoying large profits on its existing plant and equipment at the
moment, but if it anticipates no profits from the sale of goods
that an *additional* investment would make possible, the firm
will make no additions to capital. Another firm may be suffering
current losses, but if it anticipates a large profit from the production of a new good, it may launch a considerable capital
expenditure.

There is a sound reason for this anticipatory quality of
investment decisions. Typically, the capital goods bought by
investment expenditures are expected to last for years and to pay
for themselves only slowly. If capital expenditures could be
recouped in a few weeks or months, or even in a matter of a
year or two, they would not be so risky and their dependence
on expectations not so great. But it is characteristic of most
capital goods that they *are* durable and have life expectancies
of ten or more years.

The decision to invest is thus always forward-looking. Even
when the stimulus to build is felt in the present, the calculations
that determine whether or not an investment will be made
necessarily concern the flow of income to the firm in the future.
These expectations are inherently much more volatile than the
current drives and desires that guide the consumer. Expectations,
whether based on guesses or forecasts, are capable of sudden and
sharp reversals of a sort rare in consumption spending. Thus in
its orientation to the future we find a main cause for the vola-
tility of investment expenditures.

## Induced Investment

One kind of profit expectation, and the investment that
stems from it, ties in closely with the analysis we have just made
of the multiplier. This is an expectation of future profit derived
from *an observed rise in current consumption spending*.

Many business firms decide to invest because they must expand their capacity to maintain a given share of a growing market. Real estate developers who build to accommodate an already visible suburban exodus, or supermarkets who build to serve a booming metropolis, or gas stations that must be built to serve a new highway, or additions to manufacturing capacity that must be made because existing facilities cannot keep up with demand—these are all examples of what we call *induced investment*.

## The Acceleration Principle

When rising consumption induces investment, we call the effect the *acceleration principle*. In many ways it resembles the multiplier effect. The multiplier describes the effect that investment has on income via consumption spending; the acceleration principle describes the effect that consumption can have on income via investment spending. When consumption is rising and plant capacity is already tight, investment is likely to be induced, and this induced investment in turn will generate still *additional* incomes through the multiplier effect. Thus the multiplier effect and the acceleration principle can interact to yield even larger "secondary" impacts than either alone. It is interesting to note that when the Council of Economic Advisers was arguing for the Kennedy tax cut before the Joint Economic Committee of the 88th Congress, they estimated that the pure multiplier effect on GNP was only a little over 2, but that the combined multiplier-accelerator effect was 3 to 4.

## A Model of the Acceleration Principle

The acceleration principle thus helps us understand further how small increases in one sector can be magnified and spread throughout the economy. But beyond that, it enlightens us to a surprising thing. Let us discover it by imagining an industry with rising sales and fully utilized equipment and, therefore, induced investment. We will assume that our industry needs a capital equipment twice as large in dollar value as its annual volume of sales, in order to produce effectively. We also assume that 10 per cent of its capital equipment wears out and is replaced each year—that is, the average machine lasts ten years. Table 7-1 gives us a model of such an industry.

In our first view of the industry, we find it in equilibrium with sales of, let us say, 100 units, capital equipment valued at 200 units, and regular replacement demand of 20 units. Now we assume that its sales rise to 120 units. To produce 120 units of goods, the firm will need (according to our assumptions) 240 units of capital. This is forty units more than it has, so it must order them. Note that its demand for capital goods now shoots from twenty units to sixty units: twenty units for replacement as before, and forty new ones. Thus investment expenditures *triple,* even though sales have risen but 20 per cent!

Now assume that in the next year sales rise further, to 130 units. How large will our firm's investment demand be? Its replacement demand will not be larger, since its new capital will not wear out for ten years. But the amount of new capital needed to handle its new sales will be only 20 units, not 40 as before. Its total investment demand has *fallen* from 60 units to 40.

Table 7-1 is the model to study, worked out a little further.

Table 7-1    A MODEL OF THE ACCELERATION PRINCIPLE

| Year | Sales | Existing capital | Needed capital (2 × sales) | Replacement | Induced new investment (2 × addition to sales) | Total investment |
|------|-------|------------------|----------------------------|-------------|------------------------------------------------|------------------|
| 1 | 100 | 200 | 200 | 20 | – | 20 |
| 2 | 120 | 200 | 240 | 20 | 40 | 60 |
| 3 | 130 | 240 | 260 | 20 | 20 | 40 |
| 4 | 135 | 260 | 270 | 20 | 10 | 30 |
| 5 | 138 | 270 | 276 | 20 | 6 | 26 |
| 6 | 140 | 276 | 280 | 20 | 4 | 24 |
| 7 | 140 | 280 | 280 | 20 | – | 20 |

What is the surprising fact here? It is that *we can have an actual fall in induced investment, though consumption is rising!* In fact, as soon as the *rate of increase* of consumption begins to fall, *the absolute amount* of induced investment declines. Thus a slowdown in the rate of improvement in sales can cause an absolute decline in the orders sent to capital goods makers. This helps us to explain how weakness can appear in some branches of the economy while prosperity seems still to be reigning in the market at large.*

There is, however, an extremely important point to bear in mind about the accelerator. *Its upward leverage usually takes effect only when an industry is operating at or near capacity.* When an industry is not near capacity, it is relatively simple for it to satisfy a larger demand for its goods by raising output on its underutilized equipment. Thus, unlike the multiplier, which yields its effects on output only when we have unemployed resources, the accelerator yields its effects only when we do *not* have unemployed capital. That is when induced investment is most likely to follow from increased consumption and when we are also most likely to suffer a decline in total investment, after an initial peak, once the rate of increase in consumption begins to taper off.

### Autonomous Investment

Not all investment is induced by prior rises in consumption. In fact, perhaps the more significant category of investment is that undertaken in the expectation of a profit to be derived from a *new* good or a *new* way of making a good. This type of investment is usually called *autonomous* investment.

In autonomous investment decisions prior trends in consumption have little or nothing to do with the decision to invest. This is particularly the case when new technologies provide the stimulus for investment. Then the question in the minds of the managers of the firm is whether the new product will create *new* demand for itself. Thus, even in the depths of the Depression, while textile output on the whole declined, investment in cer-

---

* We might also note that if we add another year to our model in which sales slip back to 130, our existing capital (280 units) will be greater by twenty units than our needed capital. That year the industry will have no new orders for capital goods and may not even make any replacements, since it can use its new machines in place of the discarded old ones. Its orders to capital goods makers will fall to zero even though its level of sales is 30 per cent higher than at the beginning. No wonder capital goods industries traditionally experience feast or famine years!

tain new products such as rayon and acetate yarns jumped by 75 per cent.

Technological advance is not, however, the only cause for autonomous investment, and therefore we cannot statistically separate autonomous from induced investment. With some economic stimuli, such as the opening of a new territory or shifts in population or population growth, the motivations of both autonomous and induced investment are undoubtedly present. Yet there is a meaningful distinction between the two, insofar as induced investment is sensitive and responsive to consumption, whereas autonomous investment is not. This means that induced investment, by its nature, is more foreseeable than autonomous investment.

At the same time, both spontaneous and induced investments are powerfully affected by the over-all investment "climate"—not alone the economic climate of confidence, the level and direction of the stock market, etc., but the political scene, international developments, and so on. Hence it is not surprising that investment becomes by far the most unpredictable of the components of GNP, and thus the key "independent" variable in any model of GNP.

## The Rate of Interest

The profit expectations that guide investment decisions are largely unpredictable. But there exists another guideline for investment decisions that works in a more determinable manner. This is the influence of the *rate of interest* on the investment decisions of business firms.

Typically, the rate of interest offers two guides to the investing firm. If the businessman must borrow capital, a higher rate of interest makes it more expensive to undertake an investment. For huge firms that target a return of 15 or 20 per cent on their investment projects, a change in the interest rate from 5 to 6 per cent may be negligible. But for certain kinds of investment—notably utilities and home construction—interest rates constitute an important component of the cost of investment funds. To these firms, the lower the cost of borrowed capital, the more the stimulus for investment.

A second guide is offered to those businessmen who are not directly seeking to borrow money for investment, but who are debating whether to invest the savings (retained earnings) of their firms. To them, the interest rate represents a standard of comparison for the returns expected from various investment projects. A businessman, looking ahead to the expected earnings of an investment, sees a series of probable returns (varying, perhaps, from year to year) stretching ahead for a more or less definite number of years into the future. He can reduce this series of expected returns to a single *rate* of return on the cost of the entire investment. This rate, which expresses the expected profitability of the investment, is called the *marginal efficiency of capital* (or the marginal efficiency of investment).

But what is the standard for an "adequate" marginal efficiency of capital? One standard is to compare this rate of expected profitability with the rate of interest.* If the marginal efficiency of capital is not higher than the rate of interest, it will hardly be worth the businessman's while to invest, since he could use his funds with less risk and at the same return by lending them out himself. The fact that his marginal efficiency of capital may be higher than the going rate of interest is no guarantee that he will invest; but if it is not higher, it is a virtual certainty that he will not invest.

## The Determinants of Investment

We have been talking about the determining factors that ultimately affect the rate of investment, the background forces to which we must turn to account for any given level of investment

---

* It should be noted that there is no one single thing called *the* rate of interest, but a whole complex of rates, depending on the risk differential among different loans. At any given moment, interest rates may range from 1 or 2 per cent for short-term government notes to 10 to 20 per cent for installment loans, etc. The businessman usually focuses on the range in this spectrum that represents the interest rate for bank loans to business enterprise. These, too, differ from bank to bank and from business to business, but the whole group of these rates tends to move up and down together.

spending (much as we turn to the habits of householders as the background force determining the level of consumption). We have found these background forces for investment are not a single variable, like a propensity to consume income, but a mixture of variables: *increases in consumption that may induce investment; expected levels of profitability of new inventions, techniques, discoveries, etc., and the marginal efficiency of capital compared with the rate of interest.*

Now we can go a step further. With a general understanding of the constellation of forces that determines investment, we can begin to understand how a particular level of output is set for the economy as a whole.

## An Investment Model

Let us begin as before, with a simple model; this time, an economy having only two sectors: consumption and investment. We dispense with government and with the export sector for reasons of clarity in exposition. It will be easy enough to reintegrate them into the model, subsequently.

Next we establish schedules for consumption and saving at different levels of investment. We have already worked with a hypothetical propensity to consume schedule, so let us merely repeat it here with a new column of figures that will represent the amount of investment spending at various levels of income.

Table 7-2    SCHEDULES OF SAVING AND INVESTMENT FOR A HYPOTHETICAL
ECONOMY
(In billions of dollars)

| Income | Consumption | Saving | Investment |
|--------|-------------|--------|------------|
| 100 | 80 | 20 | 28 |
| 110 | 87 | 23 | 28 |
| 120 | 92 | 28 | 28 |
| 130 | 95 | 35 | 28 |
| 140 | 97 | 43 | 28 |

From our previous discussion, we have seen that there is no simple functional relation between income and investment, but rather that many forces bear on the investment total. We could, for instance, imagine an investment schedule that rose with income (perhaps due to the accelerator) or one that fell because expectations turned sour. In our model, for the sake of simplicity, we have assumed a schedule of investment expenditures that remains constant. The subsequent analysis would be more difficult but not fundamentally different if we used a variable schedule.

## The Interplay of Saving and Investment

If we now look at the last two columns for Saving and Investment, we can see a powerful cross play that will characterize our model economy at different levels of income, for the forces of investment and saving will not be in balance at all levels. At some levels, the propensity to save will outrun the act of purposeful investment; at others, the motivations to save will be less than the investment expenditures made by business firms. In fact, our model shows that at only one level of income—120—will the savings and investment schedules coincide.

What does it mean when intended savings are greater than the flow of intended investment? It means that people are *trying* to save out of their given incomes a larger amount than businessmen are willing to invest. Now if we think back to the exposition of the economy in equilibrium, it will be clear what the result must be. The economy cannot maintain a closed circuit of income and expenditure if savings are larger than investment (or if investment is smaller than savings). This will simply give rise to a demand gap, the dangerous repercussions of which we have already mentioned.

But a similar lack of equilibrium results if intended savings are less than intended investment expenditure (or if investment spending is greater than the propensity to save). Now businessmen will be pumping out more than enough to offset the savings gap. The additional expenditures, over and above those that compensate for saving, will flow into the economy to create new incomes—and out of those new incomes, new savings.

*Income will be stable, in other words, only when the flow of intended investment just compensates for the flow of intended saving.* Investment and saving thus conduct a tug of war around this pivot point, driving the economy upward when intended investment exceeds the flow of intended saving; downward when it fails to offset saving.*

## The Idea of Equilibrium

But how will the pivot point be determined? How do we know at what level of income saving and investment schedules will converge?

A diagram may once again help to clarify the point. Here is one that resembles the scatter diagram on page 72 but is, in fact, somewhat different. Note first the quantities that we are representing along the two axes. On the vertical axis we measure the total amount of *expenditure* in our simple economy, or $C + I$. Along the horizontal axis, we measure the total amount of *income* and its disposition, or $C + S$. Diagram 7-1 shows these two basic categories of measurement. Any point on this diagram will therefore indicate a certain level of spending (the distance from the horizontal axis) and a certain level of income (the distance to the right of the vertical axis).

To our diagram we now add the familiar propensity to con-

---

* The careful reader may have noticed that we speak of *intended* savings or of *intended* investments. This is because there is a formal balance between *all* saving and *all* investment in the economy at every instant. After all, saving and investment are only different names for the portion of economic output that is not consumed: from one point of view, this portion is "saved"; from another, it is "invested." But this strict balance between saving and investment is of no more analytic interest than the fact that both sides of a balance sheet always balance, whether a firm is making money or losing it. What matters in the determination of GNP are the *actions* people are taking—actions leading them to try to save, or actions leading them to seek to invest. These are the activities that must be brought into balance—and that will drive the economy upward or downward when they are out of balance. Meanwhile, a formal balance of saving and investment will be maintained because there will be temporary *unintended* saving (for instance, unexpected profits) or *unintended* investment (such as inventories that pile up or become depleted, not on purpose, but because business took an unexpected turn). These unintended items can provide our "balance sheet equality" of S and I, but they are important in dynamic analysis only insofar as they affect the powerful currents of our propensity to save and of our willingness to invest.

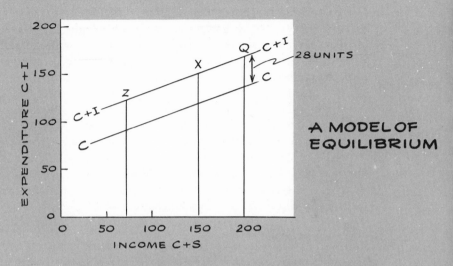

FIG. 7-1

sume schedule, marked *CC,* and on top of that (28 units higher, as our schedules in Table 7-2 on p. 100 show) the schedule for investment. The consumption and the investment schedules added together give us the line marked $C + I$.

What will be the pivot point, the equilibrium income, given this schedule of investment desires and of the propensity to consume? Obviously, it must be at that point *where the amount of income received is just equal to the amount spent.* On our diagram, this is at the point $X$ on the equilibrium line. Dropping to our income axis, we measure it to be about $150 billions.

Why is this an equilibrium level for income? Well, we know that the equilibrium level must be at *some* point along the $C + I$ schedule, for income in our model economy is simply the sum of $C + I$. Suppose that we chose point $Z$, to the left of $X$, as our pivot point. If we measure the location of point $Z$ on the vertical axis, we can see that it lies at around 125. On the horizontal axis, on the other hand, it measures at less than 75. What this says is that over 125 units of income have been pumped out by $C + I$ expenditures, but less than 75 units of income have been accounted for as $C + S$! Something is obviously amiss. The same imbalance would of course be true if we chose a point to the right of $X$, such as $Q$. Now we can see that over 200 units of income have been received (and used for consumption or saving) but that less than 175 units of income have been expended. Obviously, this cannot be an equilibrium point, either. There is a quick way of finding where the equilibrium income will be. If the reader will pencil in a line on Fig. 7-1, running upward and to the right at 45° from the meeting point of the two axes, he will find that the equilibrium income lies directly on this line. This is so because the line merely shows us all the points on the chart where expenditures $(C + I)$ equal income $(C + S)$.

## A New Equilibrium

Thus, given our investment schedule and our saving schedule, we see that there is one and only one equilibrium level at which income must settle. But this equilibrium need not be maintained. Suppose investment intentions now increase and that business firms spend *another* 28 billions for investment. Our line $C + I$ changes to $C + I'$, as shown in Fig. 7-2. Now what happens?

By using the shortcut method of the 45° line (which is shown on this diagram), we see that the equilibrium income for the $C + I'$ schedule, shown by the broken line, lies at $X'$. If we now measure the amount of income represented by this new equilibrium point, we find it to be 200.

Here is a puzzle. We have increased our investment expenditure by 28. But our income has risen by 50. How can this be?

The answer lies in our now familiar multiplier. The increase of 28 in investment spending has brought about a *larger* increase in income because of the respending of the original additional income.

How much larger? That depends, of course, on the marginal propensity to save (or its complement, the marginal propensity

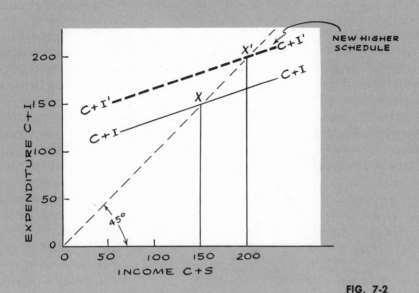

FIG. 7-2

to consume). The importance of this crucial pattern of behavior is demonstrated in our next diagram. In Fig. 7-3 we see the effect of the *same* increase in investment with two different marginal propensities to consume—which is to say, two different multipliers. We can imagine the diagram as showing the difference between two nations: both have the same national income, but one has a much higher marginal propensity to consume than the other.

We read the diagram by beginning at equilibrium point X. Through this point pass the combined consumption plus investment schedules of the two nations: $C_1 + I$, a country with high marginal propensity to consume, and $C_2 + I$, a country with a low mpc.

Now let us assume that investment in each country increases by the same amount, with the result that the schedules leap from their original position to the higher positions shown by the

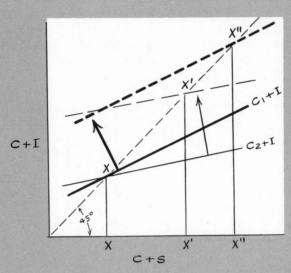

**FIG. 7-3**

broken line parallel to each. Note how much further to the right is $X''$, the new equilibrium income of the high mpc nation, than $X'$, the new equilibrium of the low mpc nation. This should not surprise us, for we already know that a high marginal consumption ratio exerts a stronger multiplier effect than a low ratio. What we see here is only the diagrammatic representation of how different marginal propensities influence the final equilibrium level of income.

### Determinants of the New Equilibrium

Thus we have begun to understand how GNP reaches an equilibrium position after a change in investment. Here it is well to remember, however, that the word "equilibrium" does not imply a static, motionless state. We use the word only to denote the fact that, *given* certain behavior patterns of consumption and investment, there will be a determinate point to which their interaction will push the level of income; and *so long as the underlying patterns of consumption and investment remain unchanged, the forces they exert will keep income at this point.*

When these forces change, so will the point of equilibrium. The level of the new equilibrium will then be determined by two empirical facts: (1) the size of the given change in investment and (2) the multiplier ratio.

This mechanism applies quite as much on the way down as on the way up. We can, that is, imagine a starting point at a higher income and ask what will be the lower stopping point for an economy in decline. The answer then hinges on (1) the size of the actual drop in investment and (2) the multiplier. The larger the original drop, and the larger its repercussions (this time in successive rounds of *loss* of income), the larger the fall in income that must occur until an equilibrium point is finally reached, where the forces in the economy once again balance.

## The Paradox of Thrift

The fact that income must finally settle at a level where the flows of intended saving and investment are equal leads to one of the most startling—and important—paradoxes of economics. This is the so-called paradox of thrift, a paradox that tells us that the *attempt to save more* may, under certain circumstances, lead to a *fall in actual saving,* whereas an attempt to spend more may lead to an actual rise in saving.

The paradox is not difficult for us to understand at this stage. An attempt to save, *when it is not matched with an equal willingness to invest,* will cause a gap in demand. This means that businessmen will not be getting back enough money to cover their costs. Hence, production will be curtailed or costs will be slashed, with the result that incomes will fall. As incomes fall, savings will also fall, because the ability to save will be reduced. Thus, by a chain of activities working their influence on income and output, the effort to increase savings may end up with an actual reduction of savings.

This frustration of individual desires is perhaps the most striking instance of a common situation in economic life, the incompatibility between some kinds of individual behavior and some collective results. An individual farmer, for instance, may produce a larger crop in order to enjoy a bigger income; but if all farmers produce bigger crops, farm prices are apt to fall so heavily that farmers end up with less income. So too, a single family may wish to save a very large fraction of its income for reasons of financial prudence; but if all families seek to save a great deal of their incomes, the result—unless investment also rises—will be a fall in expenditure and a common failure to realize savings objectives. The paradox of thrift, in other words, teaches us that the freedom of behavior available to a few individuals cannot always be generalized to all individuals.

*A Note on the Export Sector*

With an initial understanding of the mechanism of equilibrium and disequilibrium behind us, we have reached a very important stage in our inquiry. The interactions of the macroeconomic variables now begin to come together and the causes and mechanics of prosperity and depression begin to reveal themselves to us.

Before we go to complete our understanding, however, we must mention, if only in passing, a sector we have largely overlooked in this book. This is the foreign sector, or more properly the sector of net exports.

If we lived in a European, South American, or Asian country, we could not be so casual in our treatment of foreign trade, for this sector constitutes the very lifeline of many, perhaps even most, countries. Our own highly self-sustained economy in which foreign trade plays only a small quantitative (although a much more important qualitative) role, is very much the exception rather than the rule.

In part, it is the relatively marginal role played by foreign trade in the American economy that allows us to treat it so cavalierly. But there is also another problem. The forces that enter into the flows of international trade are much more complex than any we have heretofore discussed. Not alone the reactions of American consumers and firms, but those of foreign consumers and firms must be taken into account. Thus comparisons between international price levels, the availability of foreign or domestic goods, credit and monetary controls, exchange rates—a whole host of "extraneous" considerations—lie at the very heart of foreign trade. To begin to unravel these interrelationships, one must study international trade as a subject in itself, and that would enlarge our book by another hundred pages. Nevertheless, we should try to understand the main impact of foreign trade on the level of GNP, even if we cannot investigate the forces and institutions of foreign trade as thoroughly as we might like.

## The Impact of Foreign Trade

We must begin by repeating that our initial overview of the economic system, with its twin streams of consumption and investment, was actually incomplete. It portrayed what we call a "closed" system, an economy with no flows of goods or services from within its borders to other nations, or from other nations to itself.

Yet such flows must, of course, be taken into account in computing our national output. Let us therefore look at a table that shows us the main streams of goods and services that cross our borders.

Table 7-3    NET EXPORT SECTOR
(In billions of dollars)

| Year | Exports | Imports | Net exports |
|------|---------|---------|-------------|
| 1929 | 7.0 | 5.9 | 1.1 |
| 1933 | 2.4 | 2.0 | 0.4 |
| 1940 | 5.4 | 3.6 | 1.8 |
| 1944 | 21.4 | 9.0 | 12.4 |
| 1960 | 26.3 | 23.3 | 3.0 |
| 1961 | 27.6 | 23.0 | 4.6 |
| 1962 | 29.2 | 25.2 | 4.0 |
| 1963 | 30.7 | 26.3 | 4.4 |

First a word of explanation. The column of exports shows the total value of all goods and services we sold to foreigners; the imports column shows the total value of all goods and services we bought from foreigners. Our last column shows the net difference between exports and imports, or how much greater was the value of the goods we sold abroad than the value we bought from abroad. This difference is called *net exports,* and it constitutes the net contribution of foreign trade to GNP.

If we think of it in terms of expenditures, it is not difficult to see what the net contribution is. When exports are sold to foreigners, their expenditures add to American incomes. Imports, on the contrary, are expenditures that we make to other countries (and hence that we do not make at home). If we add the foreign expenditures made here and subtract the domestic expenditures made abroad, we will have left a net figure that will show the contribution (if any) made by foreigners to GNP.

What is the impact of this net expenditure on GNP? It is much the same as net private domestic investment. If we have a rising net foreign trade balance, we will have a net increase in spending in the economy. And this increase in spending, just like that arising from the addition of plant or equipment, will exert a magnified impact on GNP via the multiplier. Conversely, if our imports rise more rapidly than our exports, so that our net foreign trade balance declines or becomes negative, our GNP would decline—not only by the drop in net exports, but by the net fall in spending again magnified by the influence of the marginal propensity to consume.

Thus we can consider the *effects* of the foreign trade sector as if it were part of the investment sector, even though the underlying forces are extremely different. At least this simplified approach will serve us in our first introduction, as we now conclude our sectoral investigation with a look at the government portion of the economy.

# 8

# *The Government Sector*

We turn now to the last of the main sources of GNP expenditure—the government. As before, we shall begin by familiarizing ourselves with the sector in cross section before we look at it historically or analytically.

How does the government sector fit into gross national product? We know a good deal about it. The government derives its regular revenues in part from the indirect taxes, duties, and other payments that constitute part of the value of total output, and in part from income taxes that it levies on individuals and firms. Its expenditures, in turn, are used in part for the employment of factors of production who turn out public goods and services, and in part for making transfer payments of various kinds. And finally, if the government's expenditures are in excess of its receipts, it must borrow the difference from the household or the business sectors or from banks. This is an activity that will occupy us during much of this chapter.

Figure 8-1 shows us how this interplay of receipts and expenditures looked in 1963.

A few facts shown by the diagram (and a few that are not) are worth emphasizing. First, note that indirect taxes, totalling

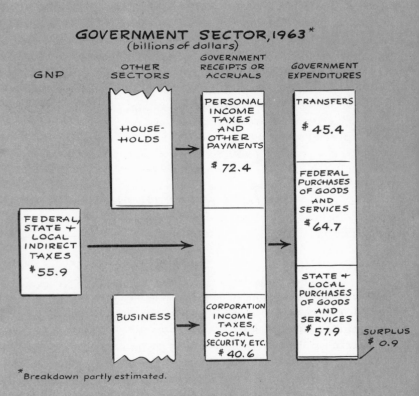

FIG. 8-1

some 56 billion in 1963, amounted to almost 10 per cent of the value of GNP. As can be seen, however, income taxes on households and business are much more important than indirect taxes in providing total government revenues. What the diagram does not show is that about two-thirds of the indirect taxes are state and local in origin: property taxes, excise taxes, motor vehicle and gasoline taxes, and others. Income taxes (and social security contributions) constitute about nine-tenths of the income of the federal government.

On the expenditure side, note that state and local purchases of goods and services are very nearly as important as federal purchases in providing public demand. Since transfer payments are largely federal in origin, however, the ratio of all federal *expenditures* (as contrasted with purchases of goods and services) to all state and local expenditures is roughly two to one.

Finally, it is worth reminding ourselves of the different significance and impact of public purchases and transfers. Public purchases of goods and services, whether they originate with local or federal government, require the use of land, labor, and capital. They are thus *public production,* and constitute a net addition to GNP. Transfer payments, on the other hand, do not increase output. They are simply a reallocation of income, from factors to various groups of the community in the business sector or the household sector. Transfers, therefore, do not require new production and are not a part of GNP.

## The Government Sector in Historical Perspective

How large does the public sector bulk in the total flow of GNP? Let us again try to put a perspective into our answer by observing the trend of government purchases over our benchmark years.

Table 8-1    THE GOVERNMENT SECTOR
(Selected years: in billions of current dollars)

| Year | Total government purchases of goods and services | Total government purchases as per cent of GNP | Federal purchases as per cent of GNP |
|---|---|---|---|
| 1929 | 8.5 | 8.1 | 1.2 |
| 1933 | 8.0 | 14.3 | 3.6 |
| 1940 | 14.1 | 14.0 | 6.2 |
| 1944 | 96.5 | 45.6 | 42.1 |
| 1960 | 99.6 | 19.8 | 10.6 |
| 1961 | 108.0 | 20.8 | 11.1 |
| 1962 | 116.3 | 20.9 | 11.3 |
| 1963 | 122.6 | 21.0 | 11.1 |

The striking change from prewar to postwar years is of course immediately visible. The government sector, taken as a whole, has changed from a very small sector to a very large one. In 1929, total government purchases of goods and services were only half of total private investment spending; in 1963, total government spending was one-and-a-half times *larger* than private investment. In terms of its contributions to GNP, government is now second only to consumption.

To make the point even more forcefully, it should be noted that Table 8-1 understates the full role of government spending, since it does not include transfer payments, but only purchases of goods and services. If we include the figure for transfer payments, the per cent of all government expenditure to GNP rises from approximately 20 per cent to almost 30 per cent. And since, as we have mentioned, the bulk of these transfers are federal (Social Security, subsidies, and interest), the per cent of all federal spending to GNP rises from 11 per cent to just under 20 per cent.

## *The Composition of Public Spending*

Thus, on the face of it, public expenditure is clearly an important source of economic activity. Nevertheless, to emphasize the rise in spending without stressing its causes would be misleading. Most of the swollen stream of federal purchases stems from defense expenditures. As Table 8-2 shows, federal *nondefense* purchases of goods and services have risen far less rapidly as a component of GNP.

Table 8-2     FEDERAL NONDEFENSE PURCHASES
(Selected years)

| Year | Per cent of GNP |
|------|-----------------|
| 1929 | 1.1 (est.) |
| 1933 | 3.3 (est.) |
| 1940 | 4.0 |
| 1944 | 0.1 |
| 1960 | 1.6 |
| 1961 | 1.7 |
| 1962 | 1.8 |
| 1963 | 1.8 |

We could also attempt to divide public expenditures into categories comparable to consumption and investment. The division is not a simple one to make, however. We would have no trouble tagging public construction for roads or airfields or dams as investment. But what are we to make of education expenditures? Economists believe that education is fully as important as capital goods for long-term growth. Shall we then count it as investment? Or what shall we make of spending on recreational facilities or on defense? The line between consumption and investment in the public sector is evidently much harder to draw than in the private sector. For reasons that we shall shortly discuss, it might be useful to list separately those items that are unquestionably additions to public capital. But since the distinction between capital and consumption in the public sphere is often unclear, economists take the line of least resistance and lump all kinds of public purchases, however varied, in one undifferentiated public sector.

## Characteristics of the Public Sector

But there is another reason why we differentiate between the private sectors and the public sector. This is the fact that the motivations of the public sector are different in a most important way from those of the private sectors.

We recall that the motivations for the household sector and the business sector are lodged in the free decisions of their respective units. Householders decide to spend or save their incomes as they wish, and we are able to construct a propensity to consume schedule only because there seem to be spending and saving patterns that emerge spontaneously from the householders themselves. Similarly, business firms exercise their own judgments on their capital expenditures, and as a result we have seen the indeterminacy and variability of investment decisions.

But when we turn to the expenditures of the public sector, we enter an entirely new area of motivation. It is no longer fixed habit or profit that determines the rate of spending, but *political decision*—that is, the collective will of the people as it is formulated and expressed through their local, state, and federal legislatures and executives.

As we shall soon see, this does not mean that government is therefore an entirely unpredictable economic force. There are regularities and patterns in the government's economic behavior, as there are in other sectors. Yet the presence of an explicit political will that can direct the income or outgo of the sector *as a whole* (especially its federal component) gives to the public sector a special significance. *This is the only sector whose expenditures and receipts are open to deliberate control.* We can exert (through public action) very important influences on the behavior of households and firms. But we cannot directly alter their economic activity in the manner that is open to us with the public sector.

## Fiscal Policy

The deliberate use of the government sector as an active economic force is a relatively new conception in economics. Like so much of the apparatus of macroeconomic analysis, it stems essentially from the work of John Maynard Keynes during the Great Depression. At that time his proposals were regarded as extremely daring, but they have become increasingly accepted by economists. Although the bold use of the economic powers of the public sector is far from commanding unanimous assent in the United States today, there is a steadily growing consensus in the use of fiscal policy—that is, the deliberate utilization of the government's taxing and spending powers—to help the stability and growth of the national economy.*

The basic idea behind modern fiscal policy is simple enough. We have seen that economic recessions have their roots in a failure of the business sector to offset the savings of the economy through sufficient investment. If savings are larger than intended investment, there will be a gap in the circuit of incomes and expenditures that can cumulate downward, at first by the effect of the multiplier, thereafter, and even more seriously, by further

---

* It is noteworthy that business groups such as the C.E.D. (Committee for Economic Development) explicitly endorse a moderate use of fiscal policy, including deficit spending, to counteract recessions. See their *Fiscal and Monetary Policy for Full Employment,* January 1962.

decreases in investment brought about by falling sales and gloomy expectations.

But if a falling GNP is caused by an inadequacy of expenditures in one sector, our analysis suggests an answer. Could not the insufficiency of spending in the business sector be offset by higher spending in another sector, the public sector? Could not the public sector serve as a supplementary avenue for the "transfer" of savings into investment?

As Fig. 8-2 shows, an expenditure gap can indeed be closed by "transferring" savings to the public sector and spending them.

The diagram shows savings in the household sector partly offset by business investment and partly by government spending. It makes clear that at least so far as the mechanics of the economic flow are concerned, the public sector can serve to offset savings equally as well as the private sector.

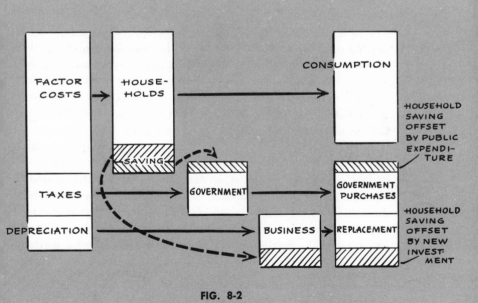

**FIG. 8-2**

How is the "transfer" accomplished? It is done much as business does it, by offering bonds that individuals or institutions can buy with their savings. Unlike business, the government cannot offer stock, for it is not run as a profit-making enterprise. However, we must note that the government can also tax incomes to finance its expenditures. To the extent that this results in less household or business spending, the government has only transferred spending from the private to the public sphere. It is likely, however, that taxes reduce private saving even more than they reduce spending. To that extent, taxation serves to "capture" savings.

### Taxes, Expenditures, and GNP

We will look more carefully into the question of how the government can serve as a kind of counterbalance for the private economy. But first we must discover something about the normal behavior of the public sector; for despite the importance of political decisions in determining the action of the public sector, and despite the multiplicity of government units and activities, we can nonetheless discern "propensities" in government spending and receiving—propensities that play their compensating role in the economy quite independently of any direct political intervention.

The reason for these propensities is that both government income and government outgo are closely tied to private activity. Government receipts are derived in the main from taxes, and taxes—direct or indirect—tend to reflect the trend of business and personal income. In fact, we can generalize about tax payments in much the same fashion as we can about consumption, describing them as a predictable function of GNP. To be sure, this assumes that tax *rates* do not change. But since rates change only infrequently, we can draw up a general schedule that relates tax receipts and the level of GNP. The schedule will show not only that taxes rise as GNP rises, but that they rise *faster* than GNP.

Why faster? Largely because of the "progressive" structure of the federal income tax. As household and business incomes rise to higher levels, the percentage "bite" of taxes increases, from around 20 per cent on the first dollar of taxable income to much higher percentages for high income brackets. Thus as incomes rise, tax liabilities rise even more. Conversely, the "propensity to tax" works downward in the opposite way. As incomes fall, taxes fall even faster, since households or businesses with lowered incomes find themselves in less steep tax brackets.

Government expenditures also show certain "propensities," which is to say, *some government spending is also functionally related to the level of GNP.* A number of government programs are directly correlated to the level of economic activity in such a way that spending *decreases* as GNP *increases,* and vice versa. For instance, unemployment benefits are naturally higher when GNP is low or falling. So are many welfare payments at the state and local level. So, too, are disbursements to farmers under various agricultural programs.

*Automatic Stabilizers*

All these automatic effects taken together are called the *automatic stabilizers* or the *built-in stabilizers* of the economy. What they add up to is an automatic government counterbalance to the private sector. As GNP falls because private spending is insufficient, taxes decline even faster and public expenditures grow, thereby automatically causing the government sector to offset the private sector to some extent. In similar fashion, as GNP rises, taxes tend to rise even faster and public expenditures decline, thereby causing the government sector to act as a brake.

The public sector therefore acts as an automatic compensator, even without direct action to alter tax or expenditure levels, pumping out more public demand when private demand is slow and curbing public demand when private demand is brisk.

How effective are the built-in stabilizers? The evidence of the 1950's suggests that they can be very helpful in preventing declines from snowballing.* If, for instance, private investment

---

* We have no evidence before the 1950's. In the prewar period, both tax income and public expenditure were too small a proportion of GNP for their stabilizing propensities to exert much influence.

were to fall by $10 billion and household spending, via the multiplier, were to threaten to fall by another $20 billion, the automatic stabilizers would ward off part of what would otherwise be a $30 billion drop in GNP. As their incomes fall, the business and household sectors will find that they owe, perhaps, $10 billion less in taxes. Of this new-found income, let us say $8 billion will be spent. Meanwhile, some public expenditures will rise, pumping, say, $5 billion into households. Together, this $13 billion, part of it direct new public spending and part of it increased consumer spending made possible by lower taxes, will act against the original decline, holding the total slump to $17 billion ($30 billion of privately induced decline less $13 billion of publicly induced expansion).

This is certainly an improvement over a situation with no stabilizers. Yet if the drop in investment is not to bring about some fall in GNP, it will have to be *fully* compensated by an equivalent increase in government spending or by a fall in taxes large enough to induce an equivalent amount of private spending. This will require public action more vigorous than that brought about automatically. Indeed, it requires that the government take on a task very different from any we have heretofore studied, the task of acting as the *deliberate* balancing mechanism of the economy.

## A Diagram of Government Spending

There is nothing in our formal analysis to make us doubt that government can take on such a task. Government spending is just like private spending so far as its multiplier effects are concerned.* In the same fashion, government taxes serve to constrict private spending, much as additional saving would.

---

* Although we should note that different kinds of private and public spending programs may have different multipliers if they go to different spending groups. A government public works program that uses unskilled labor is not apt to have the same initial repercussions on GNP as a private investment project in computers. *Transfer* expenditures may also have initial multiplier effects different from direct purchases of goods and services. And finally, different tax structures will cause changes in GNP to affect private spending differently.

Hence we can draw a new diagram showing an equilibrium for an economy with various levels of public expenditure. In Fig. 8-3, we enlarge the familiar chart from the last chapter to include a new item on the expenditure axis—government purchases, or *G*—and a new item on the receipts or income axis—taxes, or *T*. Once again we draw our 45° slanting line and our schedule of income possibilities, this time as consumption plus investment plus government purchases $(C + I + G)$.* Our new

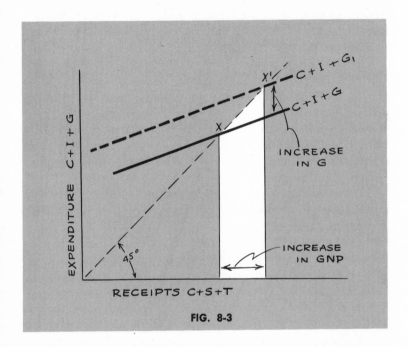

**FIG. 8-3**

---

* Although we do not show it on the diagram, as we add government expenditures and taxation to our model, we must expect the slope of the previous propensity to consume schedule to change. We should picture the impact of taxes as reducing the slope of the curve, since rising income means even faster rising taxes. On the other hand, government expenditure may redistribute income away from savers toward spenders. Hence, one cannot generalize about the way in which the addition of *G* affects the slope of the propensity to consume schedule. The effect will vary according to the tax and expenditure programs. But it is well to bear this qualification in mind.

schedule shows an equilibrium point at $X$, where all receipts, public or private, balance all expenditures, public or private.

Now let us imagine that $C$ and $I$ remain unchanged but that the regular flow of government purchasing increases, raising total outlays from $C + I + G$ to $C + I + G'$, shown by the broken line. Our equilibrium point now shifts to $X'$. Once again we note that *the change in equilibrium income is greater than the change in initial expenditure.* The reason is, of course, the same as in the case with private investment. All additional injections of expenditure into the economy will exert a multiple income effect as they pass through successive (albeit diminishing) rounds of receipt and re-expenditure.

### Deficit Spending

Thus from an analytic standpoint we can treat the contribution of government very much as if it were investment. Our diagrams of the sectoral flows and intersectoral relationships make it perfectly plain that the government sector can offset saving just as efficiently as the business sector can, from the point of view of maintaining an unbroken circuit of spending.

Yet the suggestion that the government deliberately exercise compensatory powers opens a new question for us to consider. The use of the government budget as a stabilizing device means that the government must be prepared to spend more than its normal tax receipts. It must purposefully plan a budget in which outgo exceeds income, leaving a negative figure called a *deficit*.

Like a business, however, a government cannot spend money it does not have in a bank account. Therefore it must *borrow* from individuals, firms, or banks in order to cover its planned deficit. Deficit spending, in other words, means the spending of borrowed money, money derived from the sale of government bonds.

### Deficits and Losses

Can the government safely run up a deficit? Let us begin to unravel this important but perplexing question by asking another: can a private business afford to run up a deficit?

There is one kind of deficit that a private business *cannot* afford: a deficit that comes from spending more money on current production than it will realize from its sale. This kind of deficit is called a *business loss;* and if losses are severe enough, a business firm will be forced to discontinue its operations.

But there is another kind of deficit, although it is not called by that name, in the operations of a private firm. This is an excess of expenditures over receipts brought about by spending money on *capital assets.* When the American Telephone and Telegraph Company and the Consolidated Edison Company use their own savings or those of the public to build a new power plant, they do not show a "loss" on their annual statement to their stockholders, even though their total expenditures on current costs and on capital may have been greater than their sales. Instead, expenditures are divided into two kinds, one relating current costs to current income, and the other relegating expenditures on capital goods to an entirely separate "capital account." Instead of calling the excess of expenditures a "deficit," they call it "investment."*

Can A.T.&T. or Consolidated Edison afford to run deficits of the latter kind indefinitely? Let us answer the question by imagining ourselves in an economic landscape with no disturbing changes in technology or in consumers' tastes, so that entrepreneurs can plan ahead with great safety. Now let us assume that in this comfortable economy, Consolidated Edison decides to build a new plant, perhaps to take care of the growing population. To finance the plant, it issues new bonds, so that its new asset is matched by a new debt.

### Debts and Assets

Now what about this debt? How long can Consolidated Edison afford to have its bonds outstanding?

The answer is—forever!

---

* Investment does not *require* a "deficit," since it can be financed out of current profits. But many expanding companies do spend more money on current and capital account than they take in through sales and thereby incur a "deficit" for at least a part of their investment.

Remember that we have assumed an economy remaining changeless in tastes and techniques, so that each year the new factory can turn out a quota of output, perfectly confident that it will be sold; and each year it can set aside a reserve for wear and tear, perfectly confident that the factory is being properly depreciated. As a result, each year the debt must be as good as the year before—no better and no worse. The bondholder is sure of getting his interest, steadily earned, and he knows that the underlying asset is being fully maintained.

Admittedly, after a certain number of years the new factory will be worn out. But if our imaginary economy remains unchanged and if depreciation accruals have been properly set aside, when the old plant gives out, an identical new one will be built from these depreciation reserves. Meanwhile, the old debt, like the old plant, will also come to an end, for debts usually run for a fixed term of years. Consolidated Edison must now pay back its debtholders in full. But how? The firm has accumulated a reserve to buy a new plant, but it has not accumulated a second reserve to repay its bondholders.

Nevertheless, the answer is simple enough. When the bonds come due in our imaginary situation, Consolidated Edison issues *new* bonds equal in value to the old ones. It then sells the new bonds and uses the new money it raises to pay off the old bondholders. When the transaction is done, a whole cycle is complete: both a new factory and a new issue of bonds exist in place of the old. Everything is exactly as it was in the first place. Furthermore, as long as this cycle can be repeated, such a debt could safely exist in perpetuity! And why not? Its underlying asset also exists, eternally renewed, in perpetuity.

### Real Corporate Debts

To be sure, not many businesses are run this way, for the obvious reason that tastes and techniques in the real world are anything but changeless. Indeed, there is every reason to believe that when a factory wears out it will *not* be replaced by another costing exactly as much and producing just the same commodity. Yet, highly stable businesses such as Consolidated Edison or A.T.&T. do, in fact, continuously "refund" their bond issues, paying off old bonds with new ones, and never "paying back" their indebtedness as a whole. A.T.&T., for instance, actually did increase its total indebtedness from $1.1 billion in 1929 to $8.6 billion in 1963. Consolidated Edison Company actually did run up its debt from $240 million in 1929 to $1.5 billion in 1963. And the credit rating of both companies today is as good as, or better than, it was in 1929.

Thus some individual enterprises that face conditions of stability similar to our imaginary situations do actually issue bonds "in perpetuity," paying back each issue when it is due, only to replace it with another (and, as we have seen, *bigger*) issue.

## Total Business Debts

Only a few very strong individual businesses can carry their debts indefinitely, but the business sector *as a whole* can easily do so. For although most individual businesses must prudently seek to retire their debts, as we look over the whole economy we can see that as one business extinguishes its debt, another is borrowing an even larger sum. Why larger? Because the *assets* of the total business sector are also steadily rising.

Table 8-3 shows this trend in the growth of corporate debt.*

Table 8-3    CORPORATE NET DEBT

| Year | (Billions of dollars) |
|------|------------------------|
| 1929 | $ 88.9 |
| 1933 | 76.9 |
| 1940 | 75.6 |
| 1944 | 94.1 |
| 1960 | 301.7 |
| 1961 | 321.5 |
| 1962 | 346.0 |
| 1963 | 371.6 (prelim.) |

* We do not show the parallel rise in new equities (shares of stock), since changes in stock market prices play so large a role here. We might, however, add a mental note to the effect that business issues new stock each year, as well as new bonds. In the 1960's, net new stock issues have ranged from about $1 to $3 billion per annum.

Note that from 1929 through 1940, corporate debt *declined*. The shrinkage coincided with the years of depression and slow recovery, when additions to capital plant were small. But beginning with the onset of the war, we see a very rapid increase in businesses indebtedness, an increase that continues down to our present day.

If we think of this creation of debt (and equity) as part of the savings–investment process, the relationship between debts and assets should be clear. Debts are claims, and we remember how claims can arise as the financial counterpart of the process of real capital formation. Thus, rising debts on capital account are a sign that assets are also increasing.* Debts (on capital account) and assets go very much hand in hand; and when we see that corporate debts are rising, we can take for granted that assets are probably rising as well. The same is true, incidentally, for the ever-rising total of consumer debts that mirror a corresponding increase in consumers' assets. As our stock of houses grows, so does our total mortgage debt; as our personal inventories of cars, washing machines, and other appliances grow, so does our outstanding consumer indebtedness.

### Government Deficits

Can government, like business, borrow "indefinitely"? The question is important enough to warrant a careful answer. Hence, let us begin by comparing government borrowing and business borrowing.

One difference that springs quickly to mind is that businesses borrow in order to acquire productive assets. That is, matching the new claims on the business sector is additional real wealth that will provide for larger output. From this additional wealth, business will also receive the income to pay interest on its debt or dividends on its stock. But what of the government? Where are its productive assets?

We have already noted that the government budget includes dams, roads, housing projects, and many other items that might

---

* It is important to emphasize the *capital account*. Debts incurred to buy capital assets are very different from those incurred to pay current expenses.

be classified as assets. During the 1960's, federal expenditures for such civil construction projects averaged about $5 billion a year. Thus the total addition to the gross public debt during the 1960's (it rose from roughly $285 billion in 1959 to $310 billion by 1964) could be construed as merely the financial counterpart of the creation of public assets.

Why is it not so considered? Mainly because, as we have seen, the peculiar character of public expenditures leads us to lump together all public spending, regardless of kind. In many European countries, however, public capital expenditures are sharply differentiated from public current expenditures. If we had such a system, the government's deficit on capital account could then be viewed as the public equivalent of business's deficit on capital account. Such a change might considerably improve the rationality of much discussion concerning the government's deficit.

### Sales vs. Taxes

But there is still a difference. Private capital enhances the earning capacity of a private business, whereas public capital, save for such assets as toll roads, do not "make money" for the public sector. Does this constitute a meaningful distinction?

We can understand, of course, why an individual business insists that its investment must be profitable. The actual money that the business will pay out in the course of making an investment will almost surely not return to the business that spent it. A shirt manufacturer, for instance, who invests in a new factory cannot hope that the men who build that factory will spend all their wages on his shirts. He knows that the money he spends through investment will soon be dissipated throughout the economy, and that it can be recaptured only through strenuous selling efforts.

Not quite so with a national government, however. Its income does not come from sales but from taxes, and those taxes reflect the general level of income of the country. Thus *any* investment money that government lays out, just because it enters the general stream of incomes, redounds to the taxing capacity or, we might say, the "earning capacity" of government.

How much will come back to the government in taxes? That depends on two main factors: the impact of government spending on income via the multiplier, and the incidence and progressivity of the tax structure. Under today's normal conditions, the government will recover about half or a little more of its expenditure.* But in any event, note that the government does not "lose" its money in the way that a business does. Whatever goes into the income stream is *available* to the government as a source of taxes; but whatever goes into the income stream is not necessarily available to any single business as a source of sales.

This reasoning helps us understand why federal finance is different from state and local government finance. An expenditure made by New York City or New York State is apt to be respent in many other areas of the country. Thus taxable incomes in New York will not, in all probability, rise to match local spending. As a result, state and local governments must look on their finances much as an individual business does.

### Internal and External Debts

This difference between the limited powers of recoupment of a single firm and the relatively limitless powers of a national government lies at the heart of the basic difference between business and government deficit spending. It helps us understand why the government has a capacity for financial operation that is inherently of a far higher order of magnitude from that of business. We can sum up this fundamental difference in the contrast between the *externality of business* debts and the *internality of national government debts.*

What do we mean by the externality of business debts? We simply mean that business firms owe their debts to someone

---

* We can make a rough estimate of the multiplier effect of additional public expenditure as 2 and of the share of an additional dollar of GNP going to federal taxes as 30 per cent (see Fig. 6-3, page 89). Thus $1 of public spending will create $2 of GNP, of which 60¢ will go back to the federal government.

distinct from themselves, whether this be bondholders or the bank from which it borrowed. Thus, to service or to pay back its debts, business must transfer funds from its own possession into the possession of outsiders. If this transfer cannot be made, if a business does not have the funds to pay its bondholders or its bank, it will go bankrupt.

The government is in a radically different position. Its bondholders, banks, and other people or institutions to whom it owes its debts belong to the same community as that whence it extracts its receipts. In other words, the government does not have to transfer its funds to an "outside" group to pay its bonds. It transfers them, instead, from some members of the national community (taxpayers) to other members of the *same* community (bondholders). The contrast is much the same as that between a family that owes a debt to another family, and a family in which the husband has borrowed money from his wife; or again between a firm that owes money to another, and a firm in which one branch has borrowed money from another. *Internal debts do not drain the resources of one community into another, but merely redistribute the claims among members of the same community.*

## Problems of a National Debt

A government cannot always borrow without trouble, however. Important and difficult problems of money management are inseparable from a large debt. More important, the people or institutions from whom taxes are collected are not always exactly the same people and institutions to whom interest is paid, so that servicing a government debt often poses problems of *redistribution of income*. For instance, if all government bonds were owned by rich people and if all government taxation were regressive (i.e., proportionately heavier on low incomes), then servicing a government debt would mean transferring income from the poor to the rich. Considerations of equity aside, this would also probably involve distributing income from spenders to savers, and would thereby intensify the problem of closing the savings gap.

In addition, a debt that a government owes to foreign citizens is *not* an internal debt. It is exactly like a debt that a corporation owes to an "outside" public, and it can involve payments that can cripple a firm.* Do not forget that the internality of debts applies only to *national* debts held as bonds by members of the same community of people whose incomes contribute to government revenues.

## Expenditures vs. Tax Cuts

Finally, we must not overlook the practical difficulties of government spending. The problem is that there is usually a long lag between the time of recognition, when the need for more public spending is first admitted, and the actual expenditure of the money itself. The time lag may, in fact, be so long—eighteen to twenty-four months—that by the time the public expenditures take effect, the condition they were supposed to remedy may have disappeared or worsened. In either case, the original government program is no longer the proper one. To counteract this difficulty, many economists have urged that the government keep a "stockpile" of approved public works, to be rapidly put into effect when needed. Numerous political and technical difficulties surround this proposal, however.

Because of the time-lag problem, interest has recently focused on another method of achieving a government deficit: a deliberate tax cut (while holding expenditures steady). Tax cuts also take time to get, though, and some economists therefore suggest that we should have flexible tax rates that could be adjusted upward or downward within limits by Presidential action to create quickly a budgetary deficit or surplus.

Tax cuts have the undoubted advantage of speed, but they also present problems. One is that some of the tax cut will undoubtedly result in higher consumer saving, so that the net effect on demand of a tax cut of $1 billion will be less than the net effect of increased expenditures of $1 billion. The other difficulty is that tax cuts are not likely to stimulate demand among those portions of the population who are most in need of help during

* About 5 per cent of the U.S. debt is held by foreigners.

a recession. On the contrary, the increased flow of private purchasing activity may well bypass the most afflicted portion of the community.

There is no reason, however, why both tax cuts and increased expenditures cannot be used jointly, the one for speedy effect and the other for purposeful social action. We should recognize, nevertheless, that increasing demand by public action is not a simple matter, but one that poses very substantial problems of its own.

## Perpetual Public Debts

These important caveats notwithstanding, can a national government have a perpetual debt even in a dynamic and changeful economy? We have seen that it can. To be sure, the debt must be constantly refunded, much as business refunds its debts, new issues of bonds replacing the old. But like the business sector, we can expect the government debt in this way to be maintained indefinitely.

Will our public debt grow indefinitely? That depends largely on what happens to our business debts and equities. If business debts and equities grow fast enough—that is, if we are creating enough assets through investment—there is no reason why government debts should grow. Government deficits, after all, are designed as *supplements* to private deficits. The rationale behind public borrowing is that it will be used only when the private sector is not providing enough expenditure to give us the GNP we need.

Nonetheless, the prospect of a rising national debt bothers many people. Some day, they say, it will have to be repaid. Is this true? It may aid us to think about the problem if we try to answer the following questions:

1. *Will public assets continue to increase?* If so, we can understand why debts grow with them, just as is the case with private debts and private assets. Conversely, if we imagine that at some future date we will have enough public assets, then public debts should cease rising, just as one day when we have enough private capital, private debts and equities will cease growing.

The reason will be simple enough: we will no longer need any more net saving or net investment. All our output will go for consumption and replacement.

2. *Can we afford to pay interest on a rising debt?* The capacity to expand debts, both public and private, depends largely on the willingness of people to lend money, and this willingness in turn reflects their confidence that they will be paid interest regularly and will have their money returned to them when their bond is due.

We have seen how refunding can take care of the repayment problem. But what about interest? With a private firm, this requires that interest costs be kept to a modest fraction of sales, so that they can easily be covered. With government, similar financial prudence requires that interest costs stay well within the taxable capacity of government. The figures in Table 8-4 give us some perspective on this problem today.

Table 8-4    DEBT AND INTEREST COSTS, 1962
(In billions of dollars)

|  | Net interest | Interest as proportionate cost |
|---|---|---|
| All corporations | 14.6 | 1.7 per cent of receipts |
| Federal government | 7.2 | { 6.8 per cent of receipts<br>{ 1.3 per cent of GNP |

It can be seen that interest is a much higher percentage of federal revenues than of corporate revenues. But there is a reason for this. Corporations are supposed to maximize their sales; the government is not supposed to maximize its tax income. Hence we must also judge the size of the federal interest cost in comparison with the size of GNP, the total tax base from which the government can draw. Finally, we should know that interest as a percentage of all federal expenditures has remained very steady in recent years, and it is actually much lower than in the 1920's, when interest costs amounted to about 20 to 30 per cent of all federal outlays.

3. *Can we afford the burden of a rising debt?* What is the

"burden" of a debt? For a firm, the question is easy to answer. It is the *cost* that must be borne by those who owe the debt. Here, of course, we are back to the externality of debts. *The burden of a debt is the obligation it imposes to pay funds from one firm or community to another.*

But we have seen that there is no such cost for an internal debt, such as that of a nation. The *cost* of the debt—that is, the taxes that must be levied to pay interest—becomes *income* to the very same community, as checks sent to bondholders for their interest income. Every penny that the debt costs our economy in taxes returns to our economy as income.

The same is also true of the principal of the debt. The debts we owe inside the nation we also *own* inside the nation—just as the I.O.U. a husband owes his wife is also an I.O.U. owned by the family; or, again, just as an amount borrowed by, and owed by, Branch A of a multibranch firm is owed to, and owned by, Branch B of the same firm.

There is a further point here. Internal debts are debts that are considered as financial *assets* within the "family." Nobody within A.T.&T. considers its debts to be part of the assets of the firm, but many thousands of people in the U.S. consider the country's debts to be their assets. Indeed, everyone who owns a government bond considers it an asset. Thus in contrast to external debts, paying back an internal debt does not "lift a burden" from a community, because no burden existed in the first place! When a corporation pays off a debt to a bank, it is rid of an obligation to an outside claimant on its property. But when a husband pays back a wife, the *family* is no richer, any more than the *firm* is better off if one branch reimburses another. So, too, with a nation. If a national debt is repaid, the national economy is not rid of an obligation to an outside claimant. We would be rid only of obligations owed to one another.

### Real Burdens

This is not to say—and the point is important—that government spending is costless. Consider for a moment the main cause of government spending over the past fifty years: the prosecution of three wars. There was surely a terrific cost to these wars in lives, health, and (in economic terms) in the use of factors of production to produce guns instead of butter. But note also that all of this cost is irrevocably and unbudgeably situated in the past. The cost of all wars is borne during the years when the wars are fought and must be measured in the destruction that was then caused and the opportunities for making civilian goods that were then missed. The debt inherited from these wars is no longer a "cost." Today it is only an instrument for the transfer of incomes within the American community.

So, too, with debts incurred to fight unemployment. The cost of unemployment is also borne once and for all at the time it occurs, and the benefits of the government spending to combat unemployment will be enjoyed (or if the spending is ill-advised, the wastes of spending will be suffered) when that spending takes place. Afterward, the debt persists as a continuing means of transferring incomes, but the debt no longer has any connection to the "cost" for which it was made.

Costs, in other words, are *missed opportunities*, potential well-being not achieved. Debts, on the other hand (when they are held within a country) only transfer purchasing power and do not involve the nation in giving up its output to anyone else.

### Indirect Effects

Does this mean that there are no disadvantages whatsoever in a large national debt?

We have talked of one possible disadvantage, that of transferring incomes from spenders to savers, or possibly of transferring purchasing power from productive groups to unproductive groups. But we must pay heed to one other problem. This is the problem a rising debt may cause indirectly, but nonetheless painfully, *if it discourages private investment.*

If government spending serves to turn business expectations downward, then for each dollar of government spending, we may find that we must allow for a dollar *less* of private investment spending. Were such to be the case, the real burden of government deficits would be the new productive resources that might have been laid down in the country but were not.

This could be a very serious, real cost of government debts, were such a reaction to be widespread and long-lasting. It may even be (we are not sure) that the long drawn-out and never entirely successful recovery from the Great Depression was caused, to a considerable extent, by the adverse psychological impact of government deficit spending on business investment intentions. Business did not understand deficit spending and interpreted it either as the entering wedge of socialism (instead of a crash program to save capitalism), or as a wastrel and a hare-brained economic scheme. To make matters worse, the amount of the government deficit (at its peak $4 billion) while large enough to frighten the business community, was not big enough to begin to exert an effective leverage on total demand, particularly under conditions of widespread unemployment and financial catastrophe.

Today, however, it is much less likely that deficit spending would be attended by a drop in private spending. A great deal that was new and frightening in thought and practice in the 1930's is today well-understood and tested. The war itself was, after all, an immense laboratory demonstration of what public spending could do for GNP. The experience of 1954, 1958, and of 1964 gives good reason to believe that deficit spending in the future will not cause a significant slowdown in private investment expenditure.

### Personal Debts and Public Debts

In view of the fact that our national debt today figures out to approximately $1,600 for every man, woman, and child, it is not surprising that we frequently hear appeals to "common sense," telling us how much better we would be without this debt, and how our grandchildren will groan under its weight.

Is this true? We have already discussed the fact that internal debts are different from external debts, but let us press the point home from a different vantage point. Suppose we decided that we would "pay off" the debt. This would mean that our government bonds would be redeemed for cash. To get the cash, we would have to tax ourselves (unless we wanted to roll the printing presses), so that what we would really be doing would be transferring money from taxpayers to bondholders.

Would that be a net gain for the nation? Consider the typical holder of a government bond—a family, a bank, or a corporation. It now holds the world's safest and most readily sold paper asset from which a regular income is obtained. After our debt is redeemed, our families, banks, and corporations will have two choices: (1) they can hold cash and get *no* income, or (2) they can invest in other securities that are slightly *less* safe. Are these investors better off? As for our grandchildren, it is true that if we pay off the debt they will not have to "carry" its weight. But to offset that, neither will they be carried by the comfortable government bonds they would otherwise have inherited. They will also be relieved from paying taxes to meet the interest on the debt. Alas, they will be relieved as well of the pleasure of depositing the green Treasury checks for interest payments that used to arrive twice a year.

## The Public Sector Again in Perspective

We have spent enough time on the question of the debt. Now we must ask what is it that close examination of the problems of government finance reveals, making them look so different from what we expect. The answer is largely that we think of the government as if it were a firm or a household, when it is actually something else. *The government is a sector;* and if we want to think clearly about it, we must compare it, not to the maxims and activities of a household or a firm, but to those of the entire consumer sector or the entire business sector.

Then we can see that the government sector plays a role not too dissimilar from that of the business sector. We have seen how businesses, through their individual decisions to add to plant and equipment, act in concert to offset the savings of consumers. The government, we now see, acts in precisely the same way, except that its decisions, rather than reflecting the behavior of innumerable entrepreneurs in a search for profit, reflect the deliberate political will of the community itself.

Persons who do not understand the intersectoral relationships of the economy like to say that business must "live within its income" and that government acts irresponsibly in failing to do so. These critics fail to see that business does *not* live within its income, but borrows the savings of other sectors, and thus typically and normally spends more than it takes in from its sales alone. By doing so, of course, it serves the invaluable function of providing an offset for saving that would otherwise create a demand gap and thereby precipitate a downward movement in economic activity.

Once this offsetting function is understood, it is not difficult to see that government, as well as business, can serve as a "spender" to offset savings, and that in the course of doing so, both government and business typically create new assets for the community.

## Public and Private Assets

Finally, we have seen something else that gives us a last insight into government spending. We have seen that the creation of earning assets is indispensable for business, because each asset constitutes the means by which an individual business seeks to recoup its own investment spending. But with the government, the definition of an "earning asset" can properly be much larger than with a business firm. The government does not need its assets to make money for itself directly, for the government's reserve arises from its capacity to tax *all* incomes. So far as the government is concerned, then, all that matters is that savings be turned into expenditures, and thereby into taxable incomes.

As a result, government can and should be motivated—even in a self-interested way—by a much wider view of the economic process than would be possible or proper for a single firm. Whereas a firm's assets are largely its capital goods, the assets of a nation are not only capital wealth but the whole productive capacity of its people. Thus government expenditures that redound to the health or well-being or education of its citizens are just as properly considered asset-building expenditures as are its expenditures on dams and roads.

## Political Problems

One last thought remains. We have seen that the government can undertake fiscal operations far beyond those of any single firm. What we have not considered are the *political dangers* that may result from such a course. Is the use of the public sector compatible with the freedom of action on which a market society is based?

Much ink has been spilled on the problem of the "mixed economy"—the economy in which the public sector undertakes some responsibilities formerly entrusted to the private sector. Unquestionably, a mixed economy produces problems of many kinds, and in our next chapters we shall have something to say about various criteria that bear on the use of the government's powers. Yet few economists today would advocate returning to an economy without a strong fiscal policy. We have come to understand that the operation of the economy depends on the interplay of the sectors, and that the public sector is the *only* one inherently and legitimately under our collective control.

We should understand as well that the idea of compensatory public finance is based on a *minimal interference* into the operations of the market economy. For what are the alternatives? One would be not to intervene at all and to allow the savings–investment balance to work itself out as the propensity to consume and the inducement to invest might dictate. The risk here is that an imbalance could well precipitate a severe and cumulative depression with unforeseeable social and political consequences. The other alternative is to penetrate directly into the decision-making activities of the economy, to enforce household or business spending in conformance with a central plan. Here the cost is plain: the severe infringement of personal economic freedom. As a means of correcting the gross mistakes of the economy without running the risks of these extremes, the compensatory use of the public spending power would seem to have much to recommend it.

## Political vs. Economic Considerations

In the end, an important distinction must be made between two kinds of judgments to be passed on government spending, one valid and one not. The valid judgments have to do with *how large the public sector should be, for what purposes it should be employed, or what techniques—such as tax cuts—are appropriate at a given time.* The public sector is rightfully subject to these judgments, where reasonable men may well differ.

The other kind of judgment concerns the "soundness" of fiscal policy itself, including in particular, deficit spending, as a means of offsetting the savings gap. Here the issue is not the size of the public sector or the purpose for which it is used, for one can have a large deficit even with a small public sector. The issue in the second case concerns only the validity of the economic principles of sectoral analysis. Here political judgments must be laid aside, and the logic of government spending as a demand-creating device must be considered on its own merits, in the light of an understanding of the macroeconomic process as a whole. Reasonable men may still differ as to the relative worth of different government measures, but on the propriety of the basic economics of public finance there should be a large area of agreement.

# 9

# *Money and Prices*

We have almost completed our study of the determinants of gross national product, and soon we can recombine the separate sectoral analyses into an over-all view of the economy. But first there is a problem that we must integrate into our picture. This is the role that money plays in fixing or changing the level of GNP, along with the other forces we have come to know.

Actually, we have been talking about money throughout our exposition. After all, one cannot discuss "expenditures" without assuming the existence of money. But what we have tacitly taken for granted is that the *quantity* of money in the economy would not exert some independent influence on the course of economic events. We have dealt with money as if it were a "veil" (as the nineteenth century Classical economists put it), through which "real" forces, such as consumers' desires or businessmen's intentions or legislators' programs, exerted their push and pull. What we want to study now is precisely this point. Is money itself an active economic force? Does the quantity of money impose a ceiling on economic expansion? Or to turn the question around, can an increase in the supply of money cause GNP to rise?

## The Quantity Equation

It is surely plausible to believe that the quantity of money must influence the level of prices if only because businessmen or consumers must have more money in order to spend more: Indeed, for many years one of the most famous equations in economics proclaimed that the amount of money could be linked directly to the price level in the economy. The equation looked like this:

$$MV = PT$$

where

$M =$ quantity of money. [We shall soon carefully study the meaning of this.]
$V =$ velocity of circulation, or the number of times per period or per year that an average dollar was spent
$P =$ the general level of prices, or a price index
$T =$ the number of transactions made in the economy in a year, or a measure of physical output

If we think about this equation, its meaning is not hard to grasp. What the quantity equation says is that *the amount of expenditure* ($M$ times $V$, or the quantity of money times the frequency of its use) *equals the amount of receipts* ($P$ times $T$, or the price of an average sale times the number of sales). What the quantity equation *seemed* to say, however, was that there was a direct *causal* connection between money and prices—that if you increased the amount of money, you would increase prices, or if you decreased the supply of money you would cause prices to fall.

## The Quantity Theory

This rather mechanical interpretation of the quantity equation would, of course, be valid, if the two other items in the equation held steady while the amount of money moved up or down. In other words, if the velocity of circulation, $V$, and the number of transactions, $T$, were assumed to be fixed, changes in $M$ would have to operate directly on $P$.

But is this true? Let us probe further into the quantity
theory by looking at changes in the quantity of money and seeing
if they are reflected by proportionally equal changes in prices.

Table 9-1    MONEY SUPPLY AND PRICES

| Year[a] | Actual money supply (billions) | Index of money supply 1929 = 100 | Index of prices[b] 1929 = 100 |
|---|---|---|---|
| 1929 | $ 26.2 | 100 | 100 |
| 1933 | 19.2 | 73 | 75 |
| 1940 | 38.7 | 148 | 83 |
| 1944 | 80.9 | 309 | 115 |
| 1960 | 141.1 | 539 | 194 |
| 1961 | 145.5 | 556 | 196 |
| 1962 | 147.6 | 564 | 198 |
| 1963 | 153.2 | 586 | 201 |

[a] As of June 30, 1929–44. As of December 30, 1960–63, seasonally adjusted.
[b] GNP implicit price deflator.

A glance at Table 9-1 answers our first question. Between
1929 and the early 1960's, the supply of money in the United
States increased nearly sixfold, while prices doubled. Clearly,
something must have happened to $V$ or to $T$ to prevent the sixfold increase in $M$ from bringing about a similar increase in $P$.
Let us see what those changes were.

*Changes in V*

Table 9-2 gives us a first clue to what is wrong with a purely
mechanical interpretation of the quantity theory. In the table, we
divide the dollar value of final output (GNP) by the existing
stock of money, to see how many times an average dollar was
used in the production of this output.* As the table shows, there

---
* Note that final output is not quite the same as $T$, which includes *all* transactions, including those for intermediate goods. But if we define $T$ so that it
embraces only *transactions that enter into final output*, $PT$ becomes a measure
of gross national product. In the same way, we can count only those expenditures that enter into GNP when we calculate $MV$. It does no violence to the
idea of the quantity theory to apply it only to final output, and it makes
statistical computation a good deal simpler.

was a very marked fall in $V$ from 1929 through the war period, and there has been a slow gradual rise since then.

Table 9-2    MONEY SUPPLY AND VELOCITY

| Year | GNP | (M) Money supply | (V) Average velocity (GNP ÷ M) |
|------|-----|------------------|-------------------------------|
| | (Billions of dollars) | | |
| 1929 | 104.4 | 26.2 | 4.0 |
| 1933 | 56.0 | 19.1 | 2.9 |
| 1940 | 100.6 | 39.7 | 2.6 |
| 1944 | 211.4 | 80.9 | 2.6 |
| 1960 | 502.6 | 141.1 | 3.6 |
| 1961 | 518.7 | 145.5 | 3.6 |
| 1962 | 556.2 | 147.6 | 3.8 |
| 1963 | 583.9 | 153.2 | 3.8 |

How do we account for this change? Why does the rate at which we spend money vary? Proponents of the quantity theory in the 1920's argued that velocity was essentially determined by people's normal spending habits and that these were not subject to radical shifts. What was wrong with this view?

It may be that in the long run, the proponents of the quantity theory were right and that there is a certain constancy about the rate at which we spend money. But experience has taught us that this constancy cannot be relied on in the short run. Changes in interest rates, as we shall discover later, can lead to slowups or speedups in our rate of spending. Drastic changes in the economic environment, such as war or depression, will bring sharp changes in the velocity of circulation. In depressed times, people will often wish to hoard and businesses will be reluctant to invest, with the result that the rate of spending falls. In wartime, patriotic exhortations to save, wartime shortages, and large increases in the supply of money, may also result in a slower average rate of money turnover, although for reasons different from those pertaining to depressions.

The rate at which we spend money, then—the length of time it takes us to get rid of our paychecks, for instance—is not an unchanging characteristic of behavior. In the short run, at any rate, as conditions change, velocity can also change, with the result that a given supply of money may give rise to a larger or smaller amount of expenditure.

## Changes in T

It is certain, then, that we cannot predict the effect of a change in $M$ on the price level simply by multiplying the stock of money by a fixed and unvarying $V$. But there is a second and even more important reason why we cannot relate the supply of money to the price level in this mechanical way. This is the role played by $T$—that is, by the volume of output.

Just as the early quantity theorists thought of $V$ as essentially unvarying, so they thought of $T$ as a relatively fixed term in the quantity equation. In the minds of nearly all economic theorists before the Depression, output was always assumed to be as large as the available resources and the supply of the factors of production would permit. While everyone was aware that there might be minor variations from this state of full output, virtually no one thought they would be of sufficient importance to matter. Hence the quantity theory implicitly assumed full employment or full output as the normal condition of the economy. With such an assumption, it was easy to picture $T$ as an unimportant term in the equation and to focus the full effect of changes in money or in money spending $(MV)$ on $P$.

The trauma of the Great Depression effectively removed the comfortable assumption that the economy "naturally" tended to full employment and output. At the bottom of the Depression, real ouput had fallen by 25 per cent in real terms—that is, after adjustment for changing price levels—and one worker out of every four in the nation was without a job. Quite aside from what the Depression taught us in other ways, it made unmistakably clear that changes in the volume of output (and employment) were of crucial importance in the over-all economic picture.

## Output and Prices

How does our modern emphasis on the variability of output and employment fit into the over-all question of money and prices? The answer is very simple, but very important. We have come to see that *the effect of more money or more spending on prices cannot be determined unless we also take into account its effect on the volume of transactions or output.*

It is not difficult to grasp the point. Let us picture an increase in spending, perhaps initiated by businessmen launching a new investment program, or by the government inaugurating a new public works project. These new expenditures will be received by many other entrepreneurs, as the multiplier mechanism spreads the new spending through the economy. But now we come to the key question. What will these entrepreneurs do with their new receipts?

It is at this point that the question of output enters. For if businessmen are operating factories or stores *at less than full capacity,* and if there is an *employable supply of labor available,* the result of their new receipts is almost certain to be an increase in output. That is, employers will take advantage of the rise in demand to produce and sell more goods and services. They may also try to raise prices and increase their profits further, but if their industries are reasonably competitive, it is doubtful that prices can be raised very much; other businessmen with idle plant will simply undercut them and take their business away. An example is provided by the period 1934 through 1940, when output increased by 50 per cent while prices rose by less than 5 per cent. The reason, of course, lay in the great amount of unemployed resources, making it easy to expand output without price increases.

Thus we reach a general conclusion of the greatest importance. *An increase in spending of any kind tends to result in more output and employment whenever it is possible to raise output.* But this is no longer true when we reach a level of high employment or very full plant utilization. Now an increase in spending *cannot* quickly lead to an increase in output, simply because the resources for more production are lacking. The result, instead, will be a rise in prices, for no firm can lose business to competitors when competitors are unable to fill additional orders. Thus the corollary of our general conclusion is that *additional spending—from any source—is inflationary when it is difficult to raise output.*

### Inflation and Public Finance

This conclusion puts a capstone on our discussion of the last chapter. For now we can see that a hitherto undiscussed but major consideration attends the question of whether or not to use the public sector as a supplement to the private sector. This is the question of whether substantially "full" employment has been reached.*

If the economy is operating at or near the point of full employment, additional net public spending will only add more $MV$ to a situation in which $T$ is already at capacity and where, therefore, $P$ will rise. But note that this conclusion attaches to more than additional *public* spending. When full employment is reached, additional spending of any kind—public or private, consumption or investment—will increase $MV$ and, given the ceiling on $T$, affect $P$.

A different conclusion is reached when there is large-scale unemployment. Now additional public (or private) spending will result not in higher prices, but in larger output and higher employment. Thus we cannot say that public spending in itself is "inflationary." Rather, we must see that *any kind of additional spending can be inflationary in a fully employed economy, and will not be inflationary in an underemployed one.*

### Full Employment vs. Underemployment

So we must distinguish between two fundamentally different situations in macroeconomics: the situation of full employment and that of underemployment. Policies that make sense when one situation obtains, make no sense at all in the other. To

---

* The definition of employment, as we shall see in Chapter 11, is far from simple, and "full" employment accordingly is a complex idea. Economists usually call employment "full" when about 96 per cent of all job-seekers are at work. Some of those still unemployed are the so-called "unemployables." Others are people who have voluntarily quit one job to search for another, people in the course of moving from one location to another, etc.

spend more in the public or the private sector is clearly a main objective for economic well-being in an underemployed economy, for more spending will lead to more output and employment. But to spend more in a fully employed economy is only to cause economic mischief, for now more spending will lead only to higher prices and not to more goods or jobs. Similarly, to balance budgets or to run a budget surplus in the public sector makes little sense when an economy is underutilized, but it is the course of wisdom when there are no idle resources to absorb additional expenditures.

It is impossible to overstress the importance of this major finding of macroeconomics. One of the main differences between contemporary economic thought and that of the past is precisely this sharp division between policies that make sense in full employment and those that make sense in conditions of underemployment. It was not that the economists of the past did not understand the tragedy of unemployment or did not wish to remedy it. It was rather that they did not see how an economy could be in *equilibrium* even though there was heavy unemployment.

The dragging years of the Great Depression taught us not only that output could fall far below the levels of full utilization, but—and perhaps this was its most intellectually unsettling feature—that an economy could be plagued with unemployed men and machines for almost a decade and yet not spontaneously generate the momentum to reabsorb them. Today we understand this condition of unemployment equilibrium, and we have devised various remedial measures to raise the equilibrium point to a satisfactory level, including, not least, additional public expenditure. But this new understanding must be balanced with a keen appreciation of its relevance to the underlying situation of employment. Remedies for an underemployed economy can be ills for a fully employed one.

## Bottlenecks

This brings us to a caution worth remarking on. The economy does not move sharply from unemployment to full employment over a clear-cut line of demarcation. On the contrary, as spending increases, general unemployment gives way at first to "tight" areas of labor in a few localities or industries, or to shortages of plant capacity in a few places. Thus "bottlenecks" are typically the first sign that we are crossing over from a condition of general, to one of only partial, unemployment.

These bottlenecks may, however, begin to exert their constricting effect before the economy as a whole can be considered in a state of healthy over-all employment. This is especially the case if the bottleneck is in a strategic industry, where a price rise may lead to increases in the costs of many other industries. Bottlenecks may thus cause the beginnings of inflationary trouble *before* the economy as a whole has absorbed its unemployed.

This poses the serious problem of choosing between a degree of price rise *or* a degree of unemployment. Indeed, the experience of the 1950's and early 1960's makes it appear that a small degree of inflation, through bottlenecks, is probably unavoidable if we wish the economy to operate at high levels of output and employment. Whether this mildly rising price level is an acceptable price for high employment is not a question that can be answered unequivocally. There is always the risk that a mild *continuous* inflation may gain dangerous momentum and take on speculative tendencies. On the other hand, there is the damage done to the social fabric by the failure to offer jobs to all who want them. The result is a difficult dilemma that requires a sensitive and strong fiscal and monetary policy to steer a wise middle course.

### The Supply of Money

We have learned this all-important point: changes in $M$, the supply of money, or $MV$, the expenditure of money, will affect prices *or* output, largely depending on the degree of unused capacity of labor and plant and equipment. But we have not yet bothered to find out much about an underlying premise of the quantity equation itself; namely, that the supply of money *can* be increased. How is $M$ increased? How do we bring about a growth or shrinkage in the amount of money the economy has available to spend?

Let us begin by defining what we mean by the supply of money. Coin and currency are certainly money. But are checks money? Are the deposits from which we draw checks money? Are savings accounts money? Stamps? Government bonds?

The answer is a somewhat arbitrary one. From the spectrum of possible candidates, we reserve the term *money* for those items used to make *expenditures*. This means that we include cash in the public's possession and checking accounts, because we pay for most things by cash or check. Surprisingly, it means that we do not count savings accounts as "money" because we do not pay for things with savings accounts. Rather, we have to draw "money" *out* of our savings accounts, in the form of cash or a check, if we want to use our savings account to make an expenditure. So, too, we have to sell government bonds to get money. Stamps can sometimes be used to make small payments, but they are too insignificant to matter. Hence, what interests us, in looking into the supply of money in the United States, is how we determine the supply of currency and checking deposits.

### Currency

Currency is the form of money most familiar to us. Yet there is a considerable mystery even about currency. Who determines how much currency there is? How is the supply of coins or bills regulated?

We often assume that the supply of currency is "set" by the government that "issues" it. Yet when we think about it, we realize that the government does not just hand out money, and certainly not coin or bills. When the government pays people, it is nearly always by check.

Then who does "fix" the amount of currency in circulation? You can answer the question by asking how you yourself determine how much currency you will carry. If you think about it, the answer is that you "cash" a check when you need more currency than you have, and you put the currency back into your checking account when you have more than you need.

What you do, everyone does. The amount of cash that the public holds at any time is no more and no less than the amount that it *wants* to hold. When it needs more—at Christmas, for instance—the public draws currency by "cashing" checks on its own checking accounts; and when Christmas is past, it returns any "extra" currency to its checking accounts.

*Thus the amount of currency we have depends in the first place on the size of our bank accounts, for we can't write checks for "cash" if our accounts will not cover them.*

Does this mean, then, that the banks have as much currency in their vaults as the total of our checking accounts? No, it does not. But to understand that, let us follow the course of some currency that we deposit in our bank for credit to our account.

### Bookkeeping Money

When you put money into a commercial bank, the bank does not hold that money for you as a pile of specially earmarked bills or as a bundle of checks made out to you from some payer. The bank takes notice of your deposit simply by crediting your "account," a bookkeeping page recording your present "balance." After the amount of the currency or check has been credited to you, the currency is put away with the bank's general store of "till money," and the checks are sent to the banks from which they came, where, of course, they will be charged against the accounts of the people who wrote them.

There is probably no misconception in economics harder to dispel than the idea that banks are warehouses stuffed with money. In point of fact, you might search as hard as you pleased in your bank, but you would find no other kind of money that was yours but a bookkeeping account in your name. This seems like a very unreal form of money, and yet, the fact that you can present a check at the teller's window and convert your bookkeeping account into cash proves that your account must nonetheless be "real."

But suppose that you and all the other depositors tried to convert your accounts into cash on the same day. You would then find something shocking. There would not be nearly enough cash in the bank's till to cover your total withdrawals. In 1963, for instance, total demand deposits in the United States amounted to about $120 billion. But the total amount of coin and currency held by the banks was only $3 billion!

At first blush, this seems like a highly dangerous state of affairs. But second thoughts are more reassuring. After all, most of us put money into a bank because we do *not* need it immediately, or because making payments in cash is a nuisance compared with making them by check. Yet, there is always the chance—more than that, the certainty—that some depositors will want *some* of their money. How much currency will the banks need then? What will be a proper "reserve" for them to hold?

## *The Federal Reserve System*

For many years, the banks themselves decided what "reserve ratio" constituted a safe proportion of currency to hold against their demand deposits (the technical name for checking accounts). Since the passage of the Federal Reserve Act in 1913, however, most commercial banks in the United States have their reserve ratios determined for them by the Federal Reserve Board. Historically, these ratios have varied between 13 and 26 per cent of demand deposits for city banks, with a somewhat smaller reserve ratio for country banks. Today, the city reserve ratio is 16½ per cent; the country ratio 12 per cent.*

Yet here is something odd! We noticed that in 1963 the total amount of deposits was $120 billion and that banks' holdings of coin and currency were only $3 billion. This is much less than 16½ per cent—or even 12 per cent—of deposits. How can this be?

## *The Banks' Bank*

The answer is that cash is not the only reserve a bank holds against deposits. It also holds as its reserve part of the checks you and other depositors have put into your account; or to be accurate, since it does not hold the actual checks themselves, it holds part of the claim on other banks represented by those checks.

---

* The Federal Reserve also sets reserve requirements for so-called "time" deposits (savings deposits). These are only 4 per cent. But do not forget, time deposits do not count—or directly serve—as "money."

Here is how this works. Suppose you deposit a check from someone who has an account in Bank B into your account in Bank A. Bank A credits your account and then presents the check to Bank B for "payment." By "payment" Bank A does not mean coin and currency, however. Instead, Bank A and Bank B settle their transaction at still *another* bank where both Bank A and Bank B have their own accounts. These are the twelve Federal Reserve Banks of the country, where all banks who are members of the Federal Reserve System (and this accounts for banks holding most of the deposits in our banking system) *must* open accounts. Thus at the Federal Reserve Bank, Bank A's account will be credited and Bank B's account will be charged, in this way moving reserves from one bank to the other.

In other words, the Federal Reserve Banks serve their member banks exactly in the same way as the member banks serve the public. Member banks automatically deposit in their Federal Reserve accounts all checks they get from other banks. As a result, banks are constantly "clearing" their checks with one another through the Federal Reserve System, because their depositors are constantly writing checks on their own banks payable to someone who banks elsewhere. Meanwhile, *the balance that each bank maintains at the Federal Reserve—that is, the claim it has on other banks—counts, equally as much as any currency, as part of its reserve against deposits.*

In 1963, therefore, when demand deposits were $120 billion and cash in the banks only $3 billion, we would expect the member banks to have had heavy accounts with the Federal Reserve Banks. And so they did—$17 billions in all. Thus, total reserves of the banks were $20 billions ($3 billion in cash plus $17 in Federal Reserve accounts), enough for legal backing of all deposits.

## Fractional Reserves

Thus we see that our banks operate on what is called *a fractional reserve system.* The size of the minimum fraction is determined by the Federal Reserve, for reasons of control that we shall shortly learn about. It is *not* determined, as we might be tempted to think, to provide a "safe" backing for our bank deposits. For under *any* fractional system if *all* depositors decided to draw out their accounts in currency and coin from all banks at the same time, the banks would be unable to meet the demand for cash and would have to close. We call this a "run" on the banking system. Needless to say, runs can be terrifying and destructive economic phenomena.*

Why, then, do we court the risk of runs, however small this risk may be? What is the benefit of a fractional banking system? To answer that, let us look into our bank again.

## Loans and Investments

Suppose its customers have given our bank $1,000,000 in deposits and that the Federal Reserve Board requirements are 20 per cent, a simpler figure to work with than the actual one. Then we know that our bank must at all times keep $200,000 either in currency or in its account with the Federal Reserve Bank.

But having taken care of that requirement, what does the bank do with the remaining deposits? If it simply lets them sit, either as cash or as checks on other banks that can be cleared through the Federal Reserve, our bank will be very "liquid," but it will have no way of making an income. Unless it charges a great deal for its checking services, it will have to go out of business.

And yet there is an obvious way for the bank to make an income, while performing a valuable service. The bank can use all the cash and check claims it does not need for its reserve to make *loans* to businessmen or families or to make financial *investments* in corporate or government bonds. It will thereby not only earn an income, but it will assist the process of business invest-

---

* A run on a *single* bank can be met by other banks lending cash. But a run on all banks far exceeds the cash resources of the community. Do not forget, however, that nowadays most accounts are insured up to $10,000 by the federal government. This makes a run highly improbable; and even if a run should occur, assures most depositors that they will eventually get their money back.

ment and government borrowing. Thus the mechanics of the banking system lead us back to the concerns at the very center of our previous analysis.

## Increasing the Supply of Money

Fractional reserves allow banks to lend or to invest in securities part of the funds that have been deposited with them. But that is not the only usefulness of the fractional reserve system. It works as well to help enlarge or diminish the supply of investible or loanable funds, as the occasion demands. Let us follow how this process works.

We start again with our bank with its $1,000,000 in deposits and its $200,000 of required reserves. All the rest, we now agree, can be lent out or put into safe bonds. Now let us assume that our bank suddenly acquires *new* deposits of $100,000 (perhaps the public simply decides to carry that much less cash and deposits it to its accounts). Our bank now has deposits of $1,100,000, but its reserves have risen to $300,000—$200,000 of former reserves plus the $100,000 of newly deposited currency. Since this is more currency than it needs, it will send most of it to its Federal Reserve Bank, where the currency will be credited to its account there, just as your bank credits your account when you deposit currency.

Our bank officers immediately realize that they have *excess* reserves. To back their deposits of $1,100,000, all they need by law is $220,000, which is $80,000 less than they actually have. The rest, the $80,000 of excess reserve, they are free to put to use in loans or investments.

And so they do. If the officers decide to use the excess reserve to buy more government bonds for the bank, they will simply write a check for $80,000 on their Federal Reserve bank account to pay the seller of the bond, and thereby acquire interest-bearing securities. More interesting, the bank officers may decide to increase their loans. When the next attractive borrower comes around, they will make use of the excess reserves to lend him

$80,000. This time, however, they will not write a check on their Federal Reserve account. Much easier. The bank will simply open an account in the borrower's name for the amount of the loan it makes to him. With the stroke of a bank officer's pen, it *creates a deposit account that never existed before,* an account secured by the loan agreement signed by the businessman and "backed" to the same extent as every other account thanks to the excess reserves the bank had previously gained.

## New Money

All this seems perfectly safe and sound. As our bank president would be the first to tell us, the bank has not lent out a penny more than it "has"—in the form of excess reserves.

Yet, if we look again, we can see that our bank, for all its caution, has *created new money!* As we know, the money in our bank consists of the total of its deposits.* Originally there were $1,000,000 in deposits. Then the bank gained $100,000 in new cash deposits. This was new money for the bank, but not new money for the economy. It was simply a swap; the public gave up currency and took checking accounts instead.

But thereafter our bank opened a new account in the amount of $80,000, the amount it was entitled to lend because of its excess reserve. *This was new money.* It was a new deposit that came from no one's else deposit. It was nothing less than the creation of new spending power.

Nor is this an end to it. The businessman in whose name the new account was opened will probably soon use his money. Businessmen do not borrow to let funds sit idle. But notice that as he spends his money, it will become the basis for still more new money, for his checks will be deposited in *other* banks that will send them to the Federal Reserve Bank for clearance, *thereby*

---

* The currency *in* the banks is counted as a reserve against those deposits and is not part of our money supply. Only the cash *outside* the banks, in the pockets of the public, counts as part of the money supply. Note that our earlier definition counted as "money" demand deposits and money outside the banks.

*gaining new reserves for themselves from the banks against which the checks were drawn.* In turn, these new reserves will make it possible to open still more new deposit accounts as banks put their enhanced lending or investing power to work. Note that the process of multiple deposit creation does not create more reserves for the system as a whole. It merely spreads the original addition to reserves among banks until it is used to its maximum effectiveness.

As Fig. 9-1 shows, much as additional spending creates additional incomes via the multiplier, so additional deposits create still more deposits via the fractional reserve system. And just as the existence of a savings fraction made each multiplier round smaller than the previous, so the existence of a reserve ratio makes each additional creation of new demand deposits smaller than before.

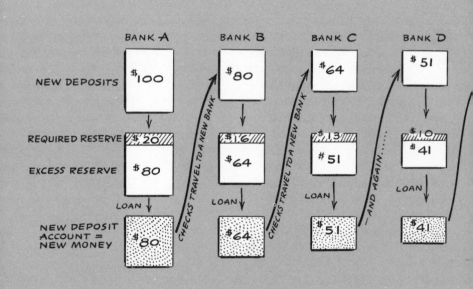

**FIG. 9-1**

In fact we can say, just as with the multiplier, that the cumulative effect of an increase in deposits will be determined by the size of the reserve ratio. If each bank must keep one-fifth of its increased deposits as reserves, then the cumulative effect of a net increase in deposits, when it has been expanded through this system, is five times the original increase. If reserves are one fourth, the expansion is limited to four times the original increase, and so on.

## Investments and Interest

Does a bank's financial investment lead to the same multiplication effect as a bank loan?

It can. When a bank buys government securities, it usually does so from a securities dealer, a professional trader in bonds. Its check (for $80,000 in our example) drawn on its account at the Federal Reserve will be made out to a dealer, who will deposit it in his bank. As a result, his bank suddenly finds itself with $80,000 in new deposits. It must keep 20 per cent of this as required reserve, but the remainder is excess reserve that it can lend or invest as it wishes. Is there a new deposit, corresponding to that of the businessman borrower? There is—the deposit of the securities dealer.

It is possible for excess reserves, albeit diminishing each time, to remain in this financial circuit for some time, moving from bank to bank as an active business is done in buying government bonds. But the very activity in bidding for government bonds is likely to raise their price, and thereby lower their rate of interest.* A lower rate of interest on bonds makes higher yielding loans to business look more attractive. Thus, sooner or later, a bank holding the $80,000 in excess reserves is apt to lend it out. Thereafter the deposit building process follows its familiar course.

---

* A bond has a *fixed* rate of return and a stated face value. If it is a 4 per cent, $100 bond, this means it will pay $4 of interest yearly. If the bond now sells on the marketplace for $110, the $4 yearly interest will be less than a 4 per cent return. If the price should fall to $90, the $4 return will be more than 4 per cent. Thus the *yield* of a bond varies inversely—in the other direction—from its market price.

## Creating Reserves

We have seen how a banking system can create money through the successive creation of excess reserves.* But the key to the process is the creation of the *original* excess reserves, for without them, the cumulative process will not be set in motion. Where do these extra reserves come from—or go to? That is the question we must turn to next.

In our example we have already met one source of changes in reserves. When the public needs less currency, and deposits its extra holdings in the banks, reserves rise, as we have seen. Contrariwise, when the public wants more currency, it depletes the banks' holdings of currency and thereby lowers their reserves. In the latter case, the banks may find that they have insufficient reserves behind their deposits. To get more currency or claims on other banks, they will have to sell securities or reduce their loans. This might put a very severe crimp in the economy. Hence, to allow bank reserves to be regulated by the public's fluctuating demand for cash would seem to be an impossible way to run our monetary system.

But we remember that bank reserves are not mainly currency; in fact, currency is a relatively minor item. Most reserves are the accounts that member banks hold at the Federal Reserve. Hence, if these accounts could somehow be increased or decreased, we could regulate the amount of reserves—and thus the

* What *is* money, really? We said before it was whatever we used to make expenditures with. But what do we use? The answer is a surprising one. We use *debts*—specifically, the debts of commercial banks. Deposits are, after all, nothing but the liabilities which banks owe their customers. Furthermore, we can see that one purpose of the banking system is to buy debts from other units in the economy, such as businesses or governments, in exchange for its own debts (which are money). What does a bank do, when it opens an account for a business to whom it has granted a loan or when it buys a government bond, but accept a debt that is *not* usable as money, in exchange for its deposit liabilities which *are* usable as money? Someone who would like to probe deeper into the curious (and very important) problem of money and how it affects our economy could do no better than to read the lucid and sparkling analysis by Peter L. Bernstein, *A Primer on Money, Banking and Gold*, Random House, N.Y. 1965.

permissible total of deposits—without regard to the public's changing need for cash.

This is precisely what the Federal Reserve System is designed to do. Essentially, the system is set up to regulate the supply of money by raising or lowering the reserves of its member banks. When these reserves are raised, member banks find themselves with excess reserves and are thus in a position to make loans and investments by which the supply of money will increase further. Conversely, when the Federal Reserve lowers the reserves of its member banks, they will no longer be able to make loans and investments, or may even have to reduce loans or get rid of investments, thereby extinguishing deposit accounts and contracting the supply of money.

## Monetary Control Mechanisms

How does the Federal Reserve raise and lower its members' reserves? There are three ways.

1. *Changing reserve requirements.* It was the Federal Reserve, itself, we will remember, that originally determined how much in reserves its member banks should hold against their deposits. Hence by changing that reserve requirement, from a given level of reserves, it can give its member banks excess reserves or can create a shortage of reserves.

In our imaginary bank we have assumed that reserves were set at 20 per cent of deposits. Suppose now that the Federal Reserve determined to low reserve requirements to 15 per cent. It would thereby automatically create extra lending or investing power for our *existing* reserves. Our bank with $1,000,000 in deposits and $200,000 in reserves could now lend or invest an additional $50,000 without any new funds coming in from depositors. On the other hand, if requirements were raised to, say, 30 per cent, we would find that our original $200,000 of reserves was $100,000 short of requirements, and we would have to curtail lending or investing until we were again in line with requirements.

Changing reserve ratios is a very effective way of freeing or contracting bank credit. But it is a massive instrument that sweeps across the entire banking system in an undiscriminating fashion. It is therefore used only rarely, when the Federal Reserve Board feels that countrywide reserves are seriously short or dangerously excessive.

2. *Changing discount rates.* A second means of control uses interest rates as the money-controlling device. Member banks that are short on reserves have a special privilege, if they wish to exercise it. They can *borrow* reserve balances from the Federal Reserve Bank itself, adding them, of course, to their regular reserve account at the Bank. The way member banks borrow is to take the government bonds they have bought and to use these as collateral, or to take the signed loan agreements they have made to their own customers and to "discount" these loans—that is, to borrow on them—from their Federal Reserve Bank.

The Federal Reserve Bank, of course, charges interest for lending reserves, and this interest is called the discount rate. By raising or lowering this rate, the Federal Reserve can make it attractive or unattractive for member banks to borrow to augment reserves. Thus in contrast with changing the reserve ratio itself, changing the discount rate is a mild device that allows each bank to decide for itself whether it wishes to increase its reserves or not.

3. *Open market operations.* Most frequently used, however, is a third technique called open market operations. This technique permits the Federal Reserve Banks to change the supply of reserves by buying or selling U.S. government bonds on the open market.

How does this work? Let us suppose that the Federal Reserve authorities wish to increase the reserves of member banks. They will begin to buy government securities from dealers in the bond market; and to pay for these bonds, they will send Federal Reserve Bank checks in the amount of their purchases to dealers.

But notice something about these checks: *they are not drawn on any commercial bank!* They are drawn on the Federal Reserve Bank, itself. The security dealer who sells the bond will, of course, deposit the "Fed's" check, as if it were any other check, in his own commercial bank; and his bank will send the Fed's check through for credit to its own account, as if it were any other check. The dealers bank will have gained reserves, although no other commercial bank has lost reserves. On balance, then, the system has more lending and investing capacity than it had before. In fact, it now has *excess* reserves, and these, as we have seen, will spread out through the system. Thus by buying bonds, the Federal Reserve has, in fact, deposited money in the accounts of its members, thereby giving them the extra reserves that it set out to create.

Conversely, if the authorities decide that the member banks have too many reserves, they will sell securities. Now the process works in reverse. Security dealers or other buyers of bonds will send their own checks on their own regular commercial banks to the Federal Reserve in payment for these bonds. This time the Fed will take the checks of its member banks and charge them against their accounts, thereby reducing their reserves. Since these checks will not find their way into another commercial bank, the system as a whole will have suffered a diminution of its reserves. By selling securities, in other words, the Federal Reserve authorities lower the Federal Reserve accounts of member banks, thereby diminishing their reserves.

## Gold and the Federal Reserve

Is there any limit to this reserve-creating or reserve-destroying power of the Federal Reserve system? There is, in a legal requirement that the Federal Reserve system must hold *gold certificates* (a special paper currency issued by the U.S. Treasury and backed 100 per cent by gold) equal to at least 25 per cent of the total of member banks' reserve balances and its own currency issue.

Here we can clear up one last mystery. What happens to the cash that the public puts into the commercial banks? And where does the public get more cash, if its demands should exceed the amount that the banks hold in their vaults? The answer again lies with the Federal Reserve. As we noted above, the amount of gold certificates that the Federal Reserve holds can be used as reserves against its member banks' deposits *or* against the actual currency it prints—the familiar Federal Reserve notes.

The rest is simple. If a commercial bank finds that it is short of cash, it "orders" some from the Federal Reserve, who charges the currency against the member bank's account (just as your bank charges your account when you cash a check). And as we have already seen, when a bank has too much currency, it can return the extra amount to the Federal Reserve, where it will be credited to its account (again, just as when you deposit currency, your account is credited).

Finally, what is the limit of the amount of paper money the Federal Reserve can print? As we have seen, gold provides the final answer. Gold certificates must equal at least one-quarter the value of member bank accounts plus Federal Reserve paper currency.

We can gain an over-all view of the monetary system by following it in Table 9-3.

Table 9-3    MONETARY SYSTEM OF THE UNITED STATES

| Unit | Held by | Required for |
|---|---|---|
| 1/35 oz gold | Treasury | $1 gold certificate |
| $1 gold certificate | Federal Reserve | Up to $4 Federal Reserve currency notes<br>or<br>$4 member bank reserves |
| $1 in member bank reserves<br>or<br>$1 in currency held by banks | Member banks (at Federal Reserve)<br>Member banks (in own vaults) | $6 worth of demand deposits (or more or less, depending on Federal Reserve regulations) |
| Demand deposits or currency outside banks | Public | Money supply |

## The Limitations of Gold

What we see here is a kind of upside-down pyramid, in which a small amount of gold at the bottom "supports" a much larger amount of money at the top. In this pyramid, the amount of gold sets an upper limit to the note-creating or reserve-creating powers of the Federal Reserve system, and in turn the Federal Reserve system circumscribes the deposit-creating capabilities of the commercial banks.

It would seem, then, that the amount of gold exercises a very important limitation on the potential monetary supply at our disposal. In mid-1964, for example, we held about $15 billion worth of gold. This meant that the total amount of Federal Reserve notes plus member bank reserves that the Federal Reserve was authorized to create was $60 billion (four times $15 billion). In point of fact, in mid-1964, there were roughly $33 billion of Federal Reserve notes in circulation, some of them undoubtedly in your pocket. This left a remainder of some $27 billion ($60 billion less $33 billion in notes) available to the system as reserves against all member bank deposits, including time deposits as well as demand deposits. In all, our gold backing came to about 29 per cent of the combined value of all Federal Reserve notes and actual member bank reserves.

A gold backing of 29 per cent, when the legal requirement is 25 per cent, might not seem to leave the Federal Reserve system much room for further expansion. Indeed, if the United States were to ship gold abroad in order to pay its international obligations, it might seem to threaten the existing supply of money with a serious squeeze.

This could indeed happen. But it is only fair to note that the gold ratio is an "ultimate" limit to our money-creating powers in name only. The ratio of gold to member bank deposits can be changed at any time by the Board of Governors of the Federal Reserve system itself, as well as by Congress. Thus if we ever found that our gold supply was too small to back the Federal Reserves liabilities, we could change the ratio of gold to member bank reserves and currency to one in five or, for that matter, to one in ten or one in one hundred. The ratio of gold to the bookkeeping entries that constitute our main kind of money is, in the final analysis, a purely arbitrary and conventional one. The real function of gold in the modern world is to serve as an acceptable means of settling up international accounts, not as a means of assuring the "soundness" of a country's money.

## Money and Expenditure

We need not delay here to learn the complex, full mechanics of a flexible monetary system. What we have seen is the basic process by which the amount of money can be raised or lowered. There remains now only one last but very important question. It is to understand exactly why a flexible monetary supply is useful and exactly how an increase in the quantity of money will affect the level of GNP.

In previous chapters of our book when we talked about GNP, we concentrated mainly on expenditure—a *flow* of spending. Money, on the other hand, involves us in the study of a *stock*—a fixed (although changeable) supply of cash and demand deposits. What does this fixed stock of money have to do with the flow of expenditure?

The answer lies in the fact that we usually need a larger stock of money to achieve a larger flow of business expenditure. If businessmen intend to increase their expenditures on investment, there is no reason to think that the existing supply of money will immediately be turned over more rapidly. On the contrary, most business money-using habits are apt to remain unchanged. As a result, businessmen who want more money to finance larger expenditures will be hard-pressed to find it. Probably they will turn to their banks for loans. But if the banks are already all "loaned up," businessmen will be able to get additional loans only by paying a higher rate of interest as an inducement for someone else to part with his money. Higher interest rates, on the other hand, are apt to *discourage* investment, as we learned in Chapter 6. Thus, having a fixed money supply could easily choke off an investment boom.

## Flexible and Inflexible Prices

There is also a second reason why a flexible money supply is needed to secure an increase in output. It hinges on the need for more money if we wish to change $T$, the volume of output. If prices were entirely flexible, if they rose and fell without difficulty, we would not need an increase in the amount of money to make possible an increase in output. In that case, as output ($T$) increased, prices would fall, and our fixed $MV$ would handle an output of any size.

But in the real world, prices are far from flexible. Many important prices are very "sticky," resistant to change, especially in a downward direction. Union leaders do not espouse wage cuts even if they know that "real" wages would be unaffected because the cost of living is falling. Many prices, such as rents, are contractual and cannot legally be changed quickly. Big firms that are relatively sheltered from the competitive marketplace tend to price goods for stability rather than for change (they even print the prices on the wrappers of many goods).

The existence of these sticky prices means that a change in the supply of money has a very important role to play in *permitting* GNP to change without falling prices. Otherwise, as output rose (and the amount of money lagged behind), consumers and business firms would simply be unable to lay their hands on the additional dollars needed to finance the larger volume of production. Consequently, we would find many goods unsold and many profit margins squeezed. As a result, investment would soon be curtailed and GNP would cease rising. Economic growth would have been stifled for sheer lack of money—not for lack of high expectations or adequate investment plans.

### Problems of Money Creation

Thus, if the supply of money were fixed, the economy would find itself in a kind of a straitjacket. With a flexible money supply, on the other hand, we can attempt to provide businessmen and consumers with bank credit just when they need it, thereby avoiding a squeeze on expansion resulting from a shortage of funds.

Nevertheless it is not always so easy to make a flexible money supply work as we would like, for there is still a gap between making more money *available* and seeing that it is *spent*. By increasing their reserves, the Federal Reserve can make it very easy for banks to make loans, but if the banks do not *wish* to make loans, as in the Depression days, there is nothing the Federal Reserve can do. Thus the dictates of private prudence (or shortsightedness) may come into conflict with the objectives of public policy—to the detriment of the latter. And even if the banks are eager to lend, businessmen may be reluctant to borrow if their profit outlook is gloomy. Some economists believe that "easy money," if continued over a long enough period, will eventually tempt businessmen into making capital expenditures. In the short run, however, we cannot be certain that this will happen.

### The Financial Demand for Money

There is as well a second reason why changes in the supply of money may not directly affect GNP as the monetary authorities wish. This is due to the fact that not all money is used for transactions purposes—that is, to carry on ordinary business expenditure. A substantial part of our money supply is used for financial purposes—not to buy materials or factors but to buy securities, or simply to serve as a liquid reserve. These financial balances are much more variable than our transactions balances. At certain times, for safety's sake or to be in a position to make advantageous purchases on the securities markets, people wish to be very "liquid"—to hold large balances in cash. At other periods, for different precautionary or speculative motives, people will be content with much smaller financial balances.

The existence of a separate financial demand for money complicates the task of money management; for holders of financial balances, whether prudence or speculation dominates their behavior, are much more prone to rapid changes in their demand for money than holders of transactions balances who must go on paying many bills, good times or bad. For instance, when interest rates are high, many holders of financial balances will seek to put their money into bonds that are selling at low prices and pay a large return. When interest rates are low, these people may prefer to enjoy the safety and potential advantageousness of liquidity, and their desire to hold cash will, therefore, rise. Indeed, from the interplay of the demand for money, arising from the public's varying *liquidity preference,* and the supply of money, as determined by the monetary authorities, will be determined the price of money or the rate of interest. In turn, as we know, the rate of interest will affect to some degree the willingness to invest. Indeed, we can think of the interest rate as a signal, showing us whether expenditures for goods and services can be financed easily or only with difficulty. Thus the public's liquidity preference plays a determining role in the economy that is quite as "basic"—although not perhaps so influential—as its behavior with regard to spending and saving.

What concerns us at the moment, however, is that a varying demand for liquidity on the part of financial holders of money can offset the actions of the Federal Reserve in tightening or loosening money for transactions purposes. The Federal Reserve may create excess reserves in the expectation that money will be pumped by bank loans into transactions balances; but if liquidity preferences are rising, the money may go instead into financial holdings. Thus an attempt by the monetary authorities to drive down the rate of interest in order to encourage investment may be frustrated if the public uses all the additional funds for liquidity and not for expenditure. In the same way, an attempt to raise interest rates and to halt price inflation by making credit tight may come to naught if the public reacts to the higher interest rates by giving up its liquidity, thereby making funds available to others to finance increased transactions expenditure.

## Problems of Timing

Thus it is not always easy to bring about a change in expenditure through a change in the money supply. But this may not be the most difficult problem of monetary management. What is perhaps more baffling is to know exactly when the economy needs an increase in expenditure. For if bank lending is encouraged at a time when bottlenecks are near at hand, more expenditure will lead only to the waste and instability of inflation. On the other hand, a failure to augment spending while idle factors are still available is to condemn some men to unemployment.

We have been plagued with problems of this sort during

recent years. Despite a slowly growing amount of unemployment, we have also had a slowly rising price level. The power of labor unions and large firms to raise wages and prices, coupled with a generally buoyant demand, has existed side by side with pockets of unemployed labor. Consequently the monetary authorities have often been on the horns of a dilemma, caught between a desire to hold back the upward creep of prices by limiting the supply of money, and a desire to expand employment by augmenting it.

Such problems may be inescapable in an economy of very large and powerful units of production and ragged and disprivileged edges to the labor force. Monetary policy cannot compensate for such disparities of economic strength or distortions of economic structure. At best, monetary policy exerts a kind of even hydraulic pressure against the entire economy. Where it fails, it reveals, as often as not, weaknesses of the environment that should be strengthened or remedied rather than deficiencies of the monetary system itself.

# 10

## *The Determination of Output*

We have completed our introduction to the various factors that bear on the determination of gross national product—the flows of consumption and investment and government spending, and the pervasive influence of money. Now it is time to recombine the elements and to review the operation of the system as a whole against a background of actual events before we move on to our last inquiry into employment and growth.

Before we come to grips with the real world, it may help if we refresh our minds with the main question we have set out to answer. The problem that has interested us has been to account, in some systematic way, for the degree of interaction of wealth and population, the two great constituents of the economic panorama. What forces regulate the flow of production that emerges from the combination of men and their natural and man-made environment? What explanations can be given for the fact that the level of output is now high, now low; that the income of the community is now increasing, now diminishing? Let us see if we can give at least partial answers to these questions.

## The Level of GNP

We begin with the over-all level of production itself, the gross national product. Can we explain why the total value of all final goods sold in the United States in 1963 was $584 billion—not $400 billion or $800 billion?

The question opens the lens of our inquiry even wider than its original panoramic focus. To find the reasons for the over-all magnitude of our economic effort requires that we look far beyond the immediate present. Only a search into the past—a search that must take into account geography, climate, religion, political customs, culture in its widest sense—can account for the present intensity of interaction between our population and its environment, or shed light on why the economic process itself has been so much more fruitful in North America than South America, or in South America than in Asia. The initial inquiry into the size (or composition) of our output must follow the route of *economic history*.

That route lies outside the ambit of this book. Our inquiry must limit itself to the growing edge of history—the present. Hence we take as "given" the quantity and quality of our population, our knowledge and inventiveness, our attitudes toward work and leisure, our stock of capital equipment. Our analysis must commence with this inheritance of the past and then go on to ask: why is today's output larger (or smaller) than yesterday's? Specifically, why was GNP in 1963 larger by $27 billion than in 1962? If we can answer that question, however imperfectly, we will at least have learned how to think constructively about the more pressing question of tomorrow's output.

## The Economic Circuit

Let us not come too quickly into contact with the future, however. It will help to clarify our thoughts if we briefly cover again the terrain over which we have come. So we turn our minds back to one of the first economic concepts that macroeconomics introduced us to—the idea of a circular flow. A circular flow economy, we recall, is an essentially stationary system, where no disturbing changes in population or taste or techniques disrupt the market, and where neither *net* saving or investment take place. We learned that in such an economy any given level of income *can* be maintained indefinitely through a continuous process of expenditure and receipt. A circular flow economy is an economic perpetual motion machine.

Needless to say, the world does not much resemble a circular flow economy. Not only do drastic changes in population and taste and technology constantly upset the market, but net saving and net investment are at the very core of the economic process. Without net saving and investment, additions to our capital stock would be impossible to achieve, and as a result, our growing population would have to work with an ever diminishing stock of capital per person.

But the idea of the circular flow taught us that even in an economy in which saving and investing were taking place, the circuit of expenditure and receipt could still be maintained. The necessary condition was only that the savings of the economy—representing purchasing power received but not immediately returned to the marketplace—be offset by expenditure elsewhere. Thus we were introduced to the idea of *offsets to saving* as the key consideration in determining whether or not a given level of income would be perpetuated.

### Sectoral Analysis

To simplify the problem of analyzing expenditures, and especially the expenditures needed to offset saving, we then divided the over-all flow of economic activity into sectors—that is, into broad categories of economic units with similar behavioral motivations and patterns in critical matters. A flow that was previously differentiated into only consumption spending and capital spending was thereby separated into four main expenditure streams: one originating with households and destined for consumer goods, one emanating from government agencies for the purchase of public goods and services, one from business firms for replacement and net investment, and a last small stream emanating from household and business and government for the net purchase or sale of goods from abroad.

If we now turn to actual GNP for 1962 and 1963, we can see these sectoral flows in Table 10-1.

Table 10-1     COMPARISON OF GNP: 1962 AND 1963

| Sector | Kind of expenditure | Billions of dollars* (1962) | (1963) | Change 1962/1963 |
|--------|--------------------|--------------------|-------|------------------|
| Household | Consumption | 356.8 | 375.0 | 18.2 |
| Business | Gross private domestic investment | 79.1 | 82.0 | 2.9 |
| Government | Public goods and services | 116.3 | 122.6 | 6.3 |
| Foreign | Net exports | 4.0 | 4.4 | 0.4 |
| All sectors | All purchases of final goods and services | 556.2 | 583.9 | 27.7 |

* Totals do not add, owing to rounding.

*Closer Analysis*

This sectoral approach is an invaluable means of simplifying the myriad events of a market economy by sorting out its buyers and sellers into a few groups with important common characteristics. If we wish to go beyond the most general analysis, however, it may simplify events too much by hiding interesting or significant eddies within the main current of the different sectors. Thus to understand the change between 1962 and 1963, we should at least break down the main sectors into their major subcomponents, as in Table 10-2.

A breakdown such as that above allows us to begin to pinpoint the locations of change in the economy. We can see that the buoyancy of consumer sales, for instance, is due in important measure to the upward trend of purchases of services and the big percentage jump in durables (this was a good year for cars). We note that the increase in investment expenditures is visible in both building and producers' equipment, and that inventories declined—a generally healthy sign. In the government sector, the surprising importance of rising state and local expenditures immediately stands out. (If we tracked down that item still further we would find a good deal of it due to higher state and local expenditures for education.)

Table 10-2   GNP BY SUBSECTOR: 1962 AND 1963
(In billions of dollars)

|  | 1962 | 1963 | Change 1962/1963 |
|---|---|---|---|
| Consumption |  |  |  |
| Durable goods | 48.4 | 52.1 | 3.7 |
| Nondurable goods | 162.0 | 167.5 | 5.5 |
| Services | 146.4 | 155.3 | 8.9 |
| Gross private domestic investment |  |  |  |
| New construction | 44.2 | 46.6 | 2.4 |
| Producers durable equipment | 29.0 | 31.0 | 2.0 |
| Change in inventories | 5.9 | 4.4 | —1.5 |
| Government purchases |  |  |  |
| Federal (defense) | 53.6 | 55.2 | 1.6 |
| Federal (other) | 9.3 | 9.5 | 0.2 |
| State and local | 53.5 | 57.9 | 4.4 |
| Net exports |  |  |  |
| Exports | 29.2 | 30.7 | 1.5 |
| Imports | 25.2 | 26.3 | 1.1 |

It would be possible to devote many pages to a detailed breakdown of the actual streams of purchasing that gave us our gross national product for the two years in question. Indeed, much of the current economic analysis to be found in the financial sections of newspapers or magazines or in the newsletters of banks or brokerage firms is precisely such an attempt to identify as closely as possible sources of additional demand or possible areas of demand deficiency.

## Dynamic Forces

But in this analysis, we want only to point out the direction that practical research can go, and then to move on. For our study of the macroeconomic process has introduced us not alone to the sectoral simplification of our total economic flow of output, but also to some of the dynamic forces that characterize each sector. Unless we understand these underlying forces we will not be able to integrate our statistical findings into a coherent whole.

For instance, does the fact that consumption increased by twice as much as all other sources of additional buying mean that higher consumer buying was therefore the *cause* of the growth in GNP? Or was higher consumer buying merely *made possible* by rising government and private investment expenditures? Our knowledge of macroeconomic theory should enable us to answer that easily enough, but the question nonetheless points up the importance of understanding the behavioral characteristics of the various sectors. Let us review in Table 10-3 what we know about them.

Table 10-3    MAIN SECTORAL CHARACTERISTICS

| Sector | Characteristic behavior | Principal stimuli for behavior |
|--------|------------------------|-------------------------------|
| Household | Mainly passive—consumption spending depends on income. (Typical sectoral behavior summarized in Propensity to Consume schedule.) | Changing levels of income coupled with attitudes toward spending or saving marginal income. Slow underlying changes in living standards and in cultural pressures |
| Business | Mainly active—investment depends on profit expectations, or marginal efficiency of capital. | New technology. Population growth. Discoveries of resources. Rate of interest. Previous rise in consumption. "Confidence" |
| Government | Partly passive, partly active. Tax revenues and public expenditures respond automatically to changes in GNP; also can be deliberately changed. | Changing levels of GNP coupled with existing tax schedules or expenditure programs. Political decisions |

This is not an exhaustive list of the dynamic factors that serve to initiate changes in the level of total national expenditure. Fluctuations in foreign trade can serve as important sources of new spending, or as a cause of decreased expenditure. Occasional spontaneous changes in household habits, so-called "buyers' strikes" or "spending sprees," can alter the flow of consumption independently of any change in income. But the table calls our attention to the fact that the sectors do not exist as mere abstractions, but as groups of human beings impelled by common motivations, aims, and pressures.

## The Role of Money

Pervading all the sectors is the influence of the supply of money—partly exercising a permissive or restrictive role, partly helping to shape investment or consumer decisions by way of changes in the interest rate.

Here the dynamic elements are two: the decisions of the monetary authorities in making new reserves available or in contracting the reserve base, and the attitude of the public with regard to liquidity. Thus part of our considerations in regard to the GNP of 1962 and 1963 will be found in the figures of Table 10-4.

Table 10-4    MONETARY INFLUENCES: 1962 AND 1963
(In billions of dollars)

|  | 1962 | 1963 |
|---|---|---|
| Money supply, adjusted | 147.6 | 153.2 |
| Total member bank reserves | 20.0 | 20.7 |
| Total bank loans and investments | 228.3 | 246.5 |
| Interest rate, high-grade corporate bonds (%) | 4.33 | 4.26 |

Table 10-4 reveals that the expansion in GNP was financed by an increase in the money supply and (as we discover if we divide GNP by the money supply) a slight rise in velocity. Total member bank reserves increased moderately as the Federal Reserve bought bonds on the open market, and member bank loans and investments increased substantially.* Finally, interest rates declined fractionally, owing to an expanding money supply and,

* The very large increase in bank loans needs a word of explanation. All through 1962, depositors in commercial banks shifted substantial funds from checking deposits into time deposits, to take advantage of high interest rates. Since the required reserve for time deposits is only 4 per cent, against 16½ per cent for demand deposits, this shift gave the banks increased lending power against their reserves, and they promptly put it to use.

evidently, the more or less stable liquidity preferences of the public.

What was the effect of these monetary developments on the price level?* Table 10-5 shows us some leading price indicators for 1963 compared with 1962.

Table 10-5    PRICE INDICES, 1963: (1962 = 100)

| | |
|---|---|
| Total gross national product | 101.5 |
| Consumers' goods | 100.9 |
| Consumers' services | 101.9 |
| Farm products | 97.9 |
| Industrial commodities | 99.9 |
| Construction | 101.9 |

We can see that small divergent movements in prices affected the economy. In some areas, such as consumers goods or basic foods, stable or even declining prices reigned, despite generally rising incomes. Elsewhere—such as in the construction industry— the increased supply of money served not only to finance increased output, but also to bring about some further degree of inflation. The statistics thus seem to indicate that bottlenecks are at hand in various places in the economy, and we are alerted to the need for a much finer search, perhaps even industry by industry, if we wish to predict the effect of a further increase in the money supply.

## The Cross Relationships

Again, however, we turn away from a promising area of empirical research to resume our systematic review of the economic forces at work. For having now highlighted once again the dynamic elements, we must remind ourselves that changes in the behavior of the sectors or in the supply of money do not exert

* In this book we have made little mention of international economic relationships, and thus we are forced to slight the problems surrounding money management insofar as it relates to the international scene. But at least the reader should be warned that there is an important, although not pivotal, chapter missing in our analytic description of the forces bearing on the determination of GNP.

their influence on the level of GNP in a direct and simple manner. Rather, a change in one element will interact with others, bringing about a magnification, or sometimes a diminution, of its impact. We should have these cross relationships clearly in mind:

1. *The multiplier.* An additional dollar of spending in the business or the government sectors will usually give rise to *more* than an additional dollar of income in the household sector. This multiplier relationship occurs because households respend their new incomes, giving rise to still additional incomes for their recipients. The size of the multiplier relation depends, we remember, on the marginal propensity to consume and on the leakage of new spending into business profits and government taxes and imports.

2. *The acceleration principle.* Under certain conditions, mainly when plants are running at full capacity, an increase in consumption will induce an increase in investment, in turn giving rise to the multiplier effect. This can further magnify the effect of a change in initial spending on ultimate GNP. More interesting, *a slowdown in the rate of increase in consumption—even though household spending as a whole is still rising in absolute amounts—can lead to a fall in induced investment.*

3. *The automatic stabilizers.* Changes in the various sectors will have a larger or smaller impact on GNP insofar as these changes are compensated to some degree by the higher public revenues and lower public expenditures that automatically follow from a rise in GNP, and the lower tax receipts and higher expenditures that accompany a fall in GNP. The degree of this counter effect will depend on the nature of established tax schedules and expenditure programs.

Unlike most of the other elements of our basic macroeconomic scheme, it is not always possible clearly to identify the cross-relations in the actual statistics. How much of the rise in investment from 1962 to 1963 was induced by rising consumption, for instance, is a matter about which we can make only educated guesses. Much easier to spot is the obvious multiplier cross-relation between the net rise in domestic and foreign investment plus government spending ($9.6 billion) and the rise in personal income ($21.6 billion). The difficulty here is to disentangle the individual components of the over-all change. How much of our higher personal incomes, for example, leaked into imports? By how much did respending swell profits or taxes? What were the relative impacts on income of defense spending or increased educational expenditures?

These questions demand highly sophisticated techniques of investigation that are far beyond the scope of this book. It is enough that we bear in mind the central fact, amply borne out by the figures, that changes in one sector can never be considered in isolation but must always be viewed as the source of changes in others.

### Background Conditions

We have nearly finished our review of the forces that determine the level of output and income. Now we must add to the active influence of the dynamic forces, amplified or muted by the various cross-relationships among them, the pervasive influence of the background conditions of the economy—mainly the presence or absence of unemployed capital and labor. On the all-important condition of high or low unemployment will depend whether the *same* behavioral forces and the *same* cross-relationships will result in larger real output and employment or merely in higher prices.

Full employment or full plant capacity are not, however, always clear-cut conditions. Rather, the economy passes from a state of surplus resources into one of tight supplies of labor and capital through a twilight zone where bottlenecks may appear in certain areas or industries.

Between 1962 and 1963, for instance, despite the presence of four million unemployed workers and of considerable industrial available capacity, prices rose, as we have noted, in a number of industries. The co-existence of such a considerable body of unemployed labor with an over-all gently rising price level calls our attention to a source of considerable economic concern during the past years—the persistent, albeit slow, inflation that has accompanied our general prosperity. There is no doubt that this condition must be ascribed in part to a lack of competitiveness, both among workers and businesses, in certain industries and areas. Thus the existence of large and growing pools of unemployed labor in West Virginia exerts virtually no effect on the high wages of auto workers in Detroit, while the presence of considerable excess capacity in the steel industry does not always lead to lowered steel prices. Such semimonopolistic islands of economic power prevent the economy from displaying an expected full output response to increased spending and lead instead to "premature" inflationary pressures. The importance of bottlenecks is thus emphasized again, especially when we seek to account for, or to predict, the course of movement of gross national product.

### Equilibrium and Disequilibrium

All these forces and relationships help us to isolate and analyze the changes in behavior and the repercussions of those changes that accounted for the rise in GNP from 1962 to 1963. But they still do not explain precisely why the level of GNP displayed a certain stability from month to month, and did not fluctuate wildly about, or jump from one level to another in a very short period of time.

To answer this question we must recall the idea of equilibrium we first developed in Chapter 7. There, working with a simple model of an economy, we learned how a point of rest would be reached, given the existing flows of intended saving and investment. We saw how changes in income would bring about changes in the flows of saving until a balance was reached between the expansionary and the deflationary pressures in the system. Implicit in that analysis was the assumption that the schedules of consumption and investment in our model were reasonably stable—that is, not subject to violent displacements due to the tensions of the saving–investment process itself.

The fact that gross national product moved slowly and steadily upward from its level of 1962 to its new level in 1963 shows that this assumption of stability of behavior was well-founded, at least for the two years we have examined. But it is well to conclude our discussion of the determination of income with a warning that this need not always be the case.

Sometimes a fall in income will not be cushioned by a normal fall in saving, but will tick off a panic reaction among householders who will try to save even more than before. If this is not met by additional government spending or private investment, what might have been a minor decline may become a serious one. Or a rise in spending that might normally taper off, owing to the higher savings associated with higher incomes, may give rise instead to a sudden race for goods. If this in turn gives the signal for a wave of speculative investment, a dangerous inflationary movement may be born.

Thus the equilibrium process, although necessary for an understanding of how the level of GNP is determined and maintained, must not blind us to the possibilities for disruptive cumulative movements that may not reach an equilibrium until large and socially costly changes in income have taken place.

### Difficulties of Forecasting

Will a point of rest always be reached? It is possible to imagine a state of affairs in which it would not; for instance, a dogged refusal of householders to give up the attempt to save, no matter what happened to their incomes. Then GNP might fall literally to the starvation point, just as it would rise to astronomic (dollar) heights if households or businesses refused to save, even though their incomes soared. In point of fact, such grotesque changes in GNP happen only in conditions of social chaos, such as the whirlwind inflations of war-torn countries, or of nations trying to develop faster than their resources permit.

But the distance from one equilibrium point to another, even in a stable nation, can be great enough under conditions of cumulative feedback to give rise to the phenomena of depression or inflation. It is, in fact, the always present *possibility* of such cumulative movements, brought about by unexpected changes in government intentions, by international events, by unforeseen psychological reactions among consumers, by volatile sentiments expressed on the stock market, by shifts in the confidence of businessmen, that makes economic forecasting so difficult.

## GNP *in Review*

Our review of the forces bearing on GNP for 1963 is not meant to be complete, but only to indicate the relevance of what we have learned to the practical concerns of economic life. Even our cursory examination of the actual events for a single year has shown us how detailed and exacting and difficult is the inquiry into current economic facts. Someone with no more than a general grasp of theory, who pretends to be qualified to give close predictions or explanations of actual economic goings-on, is making a very rash claim indeed.

At the same time, our review has also served to point out that we are hopeless before a mass of facts, unless we can organize them with the help of theory. Indeed, the whole purpose of our macroeconomic inquiry has been to give us a basic understanding of structures and connections that would enable us to interpret, however cautiously, the facts and figures that abound in the newspapers and magazines and financial literature. One need not be a professional economist to be able to understand the thrust of the major forces in the American economy, or to assess correctly the upward and downward pressures that will result from large visible changes in the main constituents of the economic process.

# 11

# *Employment and Output*

We have reached a point in our investigations where we can now understand the forces that give rise to the flow of production. To that extent we have completed one long stage of our journey into macroeconomics. But our journey is not yet complete. We have concerned ourselves heretofore almost entirely with output in real or money terms, but we have almost entirely disregarded one crucial aspect of the real world: employment. In other words, we may now be able to give a general answer to the question of how GNP is determined, but we cannot as yet answer the equally important query: how is employment determined? How many people will be employed if GNP is of such-and-such a size? What are the forces that work for more or less employment? Until we can come to grips with these problems, we have not fully answered the very questions that impelled us originally on our investigation.

*Population and Output*

As before, let us begin by becoming acquainted with the main outlines of the problem in the past and present. In Table 11-1, we trace some of the trends in employment over a span of years—a longer span than previously examined, for some of our employment statistics need a deep perspective.

Table 11-1    U.S. POPULATION AND EMPLOYMENT
(Selected years)

| Year | Population 14 years old and over (millions) | Civilian employment | Per cent employed |
|------|---------------------------------------------|---------------------|-------------------|
| 1890 | 42  | 22 | 52 |
| 1929 | 88  | 48 | 55 |
| 1933 | 93  | 39 | 42 |
| 1940 | 102 | 48 | 47 |
| 1944 | 106 | 54 | 51 |
| 1960 | 125 | 67 | 54 |
| 1961 | 128 | 67 | 52 |
| 1962 | 130 | 68 | 52 |
| 1963 | 132 | 69 | 52 |

We note first the long rise in the population aged 14 and over, paralleled by a rising total of civilian employment. Indeed, what is striking *is* the parallelism of the two series. Despite a few years that depart from the main trend—primarily the Depression years—the over-all impression is one of great stability.

What is it that determines this basic ratio of employment to working-age population? The answer is by no means a simple one, but we can approach it by the time-honored analytic method of economics: supply and demand. Hence, let us first consider those forces that affect the willingness of the population to supply its services in employment, and then the forces that stimulate demand for that labor.

## The Labor Participation Rate

What is it that makes people want to work? In very simple, poor societies—such as those embracing the great majority of the world's population today—the question is scarcely difficult to answer. It is direct hunger and unambiguous need that drives the peasant and his wife and children to the unremitting toil characteristic of much of life in the underdeveloped world. When people are very poor, they must work to survive, whether they want to or not.

But we cannot answer so simply when we come to a nation whose standard of living is well above subsistence. Now highly complex considerations enter into the decision to work with the result that the number of people seeking employment can vary considerably. Table 11-2 shows some of these changes in various

Table 11-2    LABOR FORCE PARTICIPATION RATES UNITED STATES
(Selected years—per cent)

| Age group | Males | | Females | | Total | |
|---|---|---|---|---|---|---|
| | 1890 | 1963 | 1890 | 1963 | 1890 | 1963 |
| 14–19 | 50.0 | 43.5 | 24.5 | 28.4 | | |
| 20–24 | 90.9 | 88.3 | 30.2 | 47.6 | | |
| 25–44 | 96.0 | 97.5 | 15.1 | 41.3 | | |
| 45–64 | 92.0 | 91.7 | 12.1 | 45.9 | | |
| 65+ | 68.3 | 28.4 | 7.6 | 9.6 | | |
| All ages (over 14) | 84.3 | 78.8 | 18.2 | 37.0 | 52.2 | 57.3 |

groups in our population over the past seventy years. Remember that the table shows the proportion of people *looking* for work, not necessarily *at* work.

The table is an interesting one. We note in the last column an over-all trend toward a higher degree of "participation"—that is, toward a larger fraction of the working-age population as a whole seeking work. But this general trend obscures the complex changes that have taken place within the labor force, as shown in the first two columns.

These are:

1. *A continuing search for work in the male 25–64 group.* Employment continues to be an economic necessity for most men who are heads of families during this time of life. It is still fair to generalize that the great majority of "able-bodied" men seek work during these years.

2. *Marked declines in labor force participation for younger and older men.* In the younger brackets, we see the drop mainly in the

college age and to a smaller extent in high school ages. This mirrors both the lessened necessity for the young to begin work early and the increased need for extended training in order to enter the labor force successfully later. The much sharper decline in older age employment reflects the rise of transfer payments, especially Social Security, and private pension plans as a means of providing income for the older person.

3. *A dramatic increase in the proportion of women seeking jobs.* This is especially noticeable in the middle years, after the children are at school or grown. This entry of women into the labor ranks reflects several factors. One is the growth of nonmanual, as contrasted with manual, jobs. Another is the growing cultural approval of working women or working wives. Still another is the release of the women from household chores, in part because of modern technology, in part because of the trend toward smaller and earlier families. And not least is the pressure within the home for a second income in order to achieve a higher standard of living.

These are not the only factors that bear on the crosscurrents of labor participation. The drift from the farm (where labor never retires) to the city and factory where it retires—or is fired— much sooner in life; the decline in the number of hours of labor per week required of a job holder; the general lengthening of life expectations; the commercialization of household tasks; the growth of general well-being—all these changes in our social and economic life bear on the decision (or the necessity) to work.

It is clear, then, that we are dealing here with a highly complex economic force. What our survey seems to show, over-all, is the evolution of a society in which employment absorbs a diminishing fraction of the day and the life of the average male, while constituting an increasing fraction of the life (but not the day) of the average woman.* Note that we talk of *employment* here, rather than of actual "labor." The shift toward a larger female labor force does not wholly represent a larger absolute amount of labor performed in the economy, but to some extent merely reflects a *transfer* of labor from within the household, where it was unpaid, to the office or factory or school where it is paid.

* Yet, because the average male lives longer today, he can expect to work more years than his father or grandfather, even though his working years will not be as large a fraction of his life span as it was of theirs.

What do these complex trends portend for the future of the employment–population ratio? Insofar as that ratio reflects the long-run supply of the population looking for work, the trends of the past seem likely to continue, at least for the foreseeable future. For 1975, the Department of Labor projects a slight further fall in participation rates for men, especially in the young and old groups. As in the past, however, this is likely to be offset by a small rise in the proportion of women looking for work, particularly in their middle and later years. The net result for men and women combined is predicted to remain virtually unchanged.

## Short-run Changes

These figures indicate the direction of persistent, albeit slow-moving, main currents within the total fraction of the population that seeks work. But when we concern ourselves with employment or unemployment on a year-to-year basis, we must also take heed of short-run shifts in and out of the active labor force. That is, while the decade-to-decade percentages reveal the gradual changes we have discussed, from one year to the next, the proportion of the population actively seeking work—particularly among young people or women—may vary sharply.

If we look into the years of the 1960's, we can see how the labor force evidences these short-run expansions and contractions.

Table 11-3

|  | 1960 | 1961 | 1962 | 1963 |
|---|---|---|---|---|
|  |  | (*millions*) |  |  |
| Number in civilian labor force | 70.6 | 71.6 | 71.8 | 72.9 |
| Civilian employment | 66.7 | 66.8 | 67.8 | 68.9 |
| Unemployment | 3.9 | 4.8 | 4.0 | 4.2 |

Notice that between 1960 and 1961, employment and unemployment *both* rose. One would think that as employment rose, unemployment would fall! Yet the same phenomenon appears between 1962 and 1963. How can this be?

The answer to the apparent paradox lies in the short-run responsiveness or *elasticity,* of the labor supply. When times are good and jobs are plentiful, more youths and women will seek work. The whole labor force will then temporarily expand; and since not all of it may find work, both employment and unemployment may show increases. The reverse is true in a year of recession. What happens then is that many will be discouraged by bad times and "withdraw" from the labor force, remaining in school or in the household. As a result, the number of unemployed will then be smaller than if the larger labor force of a boom year had continued actively looking for work.

## The Meaning of Unemployment

The concept of a variable participation rate (or an elastic supply) for labor in the short run helps to elucidate for us a term with which we shall be much involved in this chapter: unemployment.

Clearly, unemployment is not a static condition, but one that varies with the participation rate itself. Technically, the measure of unemployment is determined by a household-to-household survey conducted each month by the Bureau of the Census among a carefully selected sample. An "unemployed" person is thereupon defined not merely as a person without a job—for perhaps such a person does not *want* a job—but as someone who is "actively" seeking work but is "unable" to find it. Since, however, the number of people who will be seeking work will rise in good times and fall in bad times, figures for any given period must be viewed with caution. A relatively low unemployment rate *may* mean only that general discouragement has driven many job seekers from the search for work. Similarly, a tendency for the unemployment rate to remain relatively steady as employment rises may only testify to an increased number of persons who have been attracted into the labor force.

These cautions by no means invalidate the concept of unemployment as meaningful; but they warn us against assuming that in measuring unemployment over time, we are measuring variations in a fixed quantity. An economist first looks at the labor participation figures and then at the unemployment rates before he judges the seriousness of the situation.

## Occupational Shifts

What can we say about the demand for labor, to match this general picture of its supply?

Let us begin by inquiring what sorts of labor our society has demanded over the last decades. Table 11-4 gives us a picture of the changing occupational structure of the economy since 1900.

Table 11-4     OCCUPATIONAL DISTRIBUTION OF LABOR FORCE: 1900–1963

|  | 1900 | 1963 |
|---|---|---|
|  | (per cent) | |
| *Managerial and professional* | | |
| Professional and technical workers | 4.1 | 12.6 |
| Managers, officials, and proprietors (nonfarm) | 5.9 | 10.9 |
| *White collar* | | |
| Clerical workers | 3.1 | 15.2 |
| Sales workers | 4.8 | 6.3 |
| *Blue collar* | | |
| Skilled workers & foremen | 10.3 | 12.6 |
| Semiskilled workers | 12.8 | 18.2 |
| Unskilled workers | 12.4 | 4.7 |
| Household and other service workers | 8.9 | 13.5 |
| *Farm* | | |
| Farmers and farm managers | 20.0 | 3.6 |
| Farm laborers | 17.6 | 2.4 |

The basic outlines of an enormous change in the *quality* of the demand for labor are readily seen. What can be described only as a massive movement out of rural, into urban, occupations marks the entire occupational spectrum. This basic shift, of the profoundest importance for the employment of the population, is given added visibility if we view it not from the vantage point of the new kinds of skills demanded—managerial, technical, white collar, against the older manual or farm skills—but from the point of view of the general areas of activity with which these occupations were concerned.

A glance at Table 11-5 gives added meaning to the shift in

the job structure, for it is apparent that a pervasive transformation has occurred in the final demands of society. An economy principally concerned with wresting goods from nature and then transforming them, or transporting them, has become increasingly a society concerned with selling or administering the activities of the relatively dwindling proportion who obtain, or fashion, or carry material wealth.*

Table 11-5    INDUSTRIAL AND AGRICULTURAL DISTRIBUTION OF EMPLOYMENT
(Per cent distribution of all employed workers)

|  | Agriculture, forests, and fisheries | Manufacturing, mining, transportation, construction, utilities | Trade, government, finance, professional and personal services |
|---|---|---|---|
| 1900 | 38.1 | 37.7 | 24.2 |
| 1962 | 8.6 | 39.7 | 51.7 |

Source: Calculated from *Historical Statistics*, p. 74 (unallocated labor omitted); also from *Hearings*, Joint Economic Committee, 88th Congress; Part I, p. 193.

What accounts for this enormous change in the nature of the productive activity of society? Mainly, we can account for it by the interaction of two factors: technology and the changing demand for goods and services.

## The Impact of Technology

Underlying the great migration from "primary" occupations through "secondary" ones into the "tertiary" service trades lies the impelling force of technology. Without the productive capacity given us by a technology that has developed in a certain sequence and form, this migration could not have taken place. In both the agricultural and the manufacturing–mining–transporting–power fields, we have experienced a startling increase in productivity, so that a dwindling manpower base can adequately provide the products required of them by society.

* It is customary to include transportation and utilities among the third or service area of activities. In this analysis, however, we group them with goods-producing or goods-handling activities, to highlight the drift into "purely" service occupations.

Agriculture presents, of course, the most extreme example of the power of technology to enhance productivity. Between 1880 and today, for instance, the time required to harvest one acre of wheat on the Great Plains has fallen from twenty hours to two. Meanwhile, the manhours needed to raise 100 bushels of corn has dropped from 147 in 1910 to four or five.* Not quite so dramatic but also far-reaching in their effect have been technological improvements in other areas. Table 11-6 shows the increase in productivity in various mining, transportation, and manufacturing activities during the past two decades.

Table 11-6     INDEX OF OUTPUT PER MAN-HOUR

| Industry | 1940 | 1960 |
|---|---|---|
| Coal mining | 100 | 231 |
| Railroad transportation | 100 | 221 |
| Basic steel (1959) | 100 | 173 |
| Paper and pulp | 100 | 145 |
| Petroleum refining | 100 | 198 |

Source: Calculated from *Statistical Abstract*, 1963, p. 238.

Finally, by way of contrast to the very great degree of technological advance in the primary and secondary occupation sectors, we must note the laggard advance in productivity in the tertiary sector of activity. Output per man-hour in trade, for instance, or in education, or in the service professions such as law or medicine, or again in domestic or personal services such as barbering or repair work, or in government, has not increased nearly so much as in the primary and secondary sectors.**

Thus we find the *uneven entry* of technology to be one main

* E. Higbee, *Farms and Farmers in an Urban Age* (New York: The Twentieth Century Fund, 1963), p. 9.
** It is only proper to note that we cannot measure productivity of output in the service sector nearly so unambiguously as in the goods sector, and there is no doubt that the *quality* of many services has increased substantially. Compare, for example, the "productivity" of a surgeon operating for appendicitis in 1900, 1930, and 1964. On the other hand, insofar as we are interested in the effect of technology in increasing the saleable output of work, there seems little doubt of its considerable superiority in the goods-producing branches of the economy.

cause behind the over-all migration of employment that we have discovered. Had we not enjoyed the enormous technical improvements in agriculture or mass production, but instead discovered vastly superior techniques of government (in the sense of increasing the man-hour output of, say, police or firemen or legislators) the distribution of employment might look very different. We shall return to this point when we discuss the question of automation. At the moment, we need only accept the unequal efficiencies of technology in the various sectors of economic activity as constituting one main cause for the change in employment patterns.

## The Influence of Demand

The differential rates of progress of technology are not, however, by themselves enough to explain the shift in employment. The fact that each farmer has become enormously much more productive than his grandfather does not explain the decline of farm employment, nor does the enhancement of manufacturing and goods-handling productivity explain the stability of the employment ratios of these sectors. To account for the impact of technology on employment we must link the changes in productivity with the nature of the demand for the products emanating from these various industries and activities.

We can see this shift in demand in Table 11-7, showing the division of national income going to various occupational sectors and their components.

What we see here is a shift working in a direction different from the impetus of technology. Note that as productivity has increased in agriculture, demand for the products of agriculture has *fallen* as a per cent of total national expenditure. In technical language, the demand for food products was not "income-elastic" —that is, it did not rise proportionately with the rise in income. The result of this confrontation of a high-powered technology by a low-powered demand was a squeeze on employment. If the existing labor force in agriculture were equipped with the more productive techniques, the consequence would be a torrent of output that would far surpass the demand of the market. Instead, the new technology was utilized to permit a smaller labor force to fulfill demand, while the now redundant farm labor was forced to look elsewhere for employment.

Table 11-7     PERCENTAGE DISTRIBUTION OF DEMAND FOR OUTPUT
(National income)

|  | 1899–1908 |  | 1960 |  |
| --- | --- | --- | --- | --- |
| Primary sector (Agriculture) | 16.7 |  | 4.4 |  |
| Secondary sector | 36.7 |  | 44.0 |  |
| Mining |  | 3.1 |  | 2.2 |
| Manufacturing |  | 18.4 |  | 28.0 |
| Construction |  | 4.5 |  | 4.7 |
| Transportation, communication, and public utilities |  | 10.7 |  | 9.1 |
| Tertiary sector | 46.5 |  | 51.6 |  |
| Trade |  | 15.3 |  | 17.7 |
| Misc. services |  | 9.6 |  | 10.8 |
| Government |  | 5.6 |  | 10.5 |
| Finance and other |  | 16.0 |  | 12.6 |

Where did it go? In part, it was directed by the shift of both technology and demand to the secondary sector. Farmers, moving to factory towns, produced trucks and tractors, thereby transferring some agricultural tasks to manufacturing. Meanwhile, as incomes rose, purchasing power that was not required for food products turned to the purchase of manufactured goods, homes, power, communication, and other things. The result was that employment rose in this sector, as Table 11-5 shows. Much more important, however, by way of its employment-offering effects, was the rise of the "tertiary" occupations. Here an elastic demand for services of various kinds and an absence of revolutionary labor-saving techniques permitted employment to increase very rapidly.

## The Evolution of Demand

What we seem to be witnessing, in these shifts, is a natural "evolution" of demand in an increasingly affluent and industrialized society. Demand appears to pass from an initial concentration on the products of the earth, to and through a focus on the products of manufacture, toward a "highest" stage where it fastens on the enjoyment of the personal services made possible by a highly productive society and on the increased need to administer the internal affairs of a complex industrial mechanism. Thus we should note that the shift in employment visible in Table 11-5, already striking enough, would be made even more so were we to transfer the growing "service" (i.e., administration and nonproduction) component in the secondary sector to the tertiary sector. In manufacturing alone, between 1950 and 1962, the nonproduction work force grew from 18 to 27 per cent of total employees.

## Employment, Demand, and Leisure

What light does this discussion of the demand for labor shed on our original inquiry into the relative stability of the population–employment ratio? The conclusion points up the importance of the shift in demand from less labor-requiring tasks to more labor-requiring tasks. Had consumers not evinced a desire for the relatively more labor-using manufactures and highly labor-intensive services, the total labor time required to provision society would have been considerably less. We would then have become an economy that mainly produced agricultural goods very efficiently—that is, with relatively little labor input—and one that had but few "demands" for labor in other occupations.

Such a society would not necessarily suffer high unemployment. It could use its agricultural productivity, in the absence of other wants, to reduce the work week drastically; and by distributing the remaining quota of necessary work among its population, it could still give employment to all who sought it. Its standard of living, would of course, be no higher than the amount of agricultural produce it would then bring forth, but this would be a voluntarily chosen standard that accorded leisure a higher value than the nonagricultural goods and services that might have been produced.

It need hardly be said that the United States is not such a society. As our productivity in primary products has confronted the stone wall of our inelastic demand for primary products, we have shifted both our wants and our labor power into the secondary and tertiary sectors. Nonetheless, so great has been the rise in productivity in primary and secondary sectors that we have also been able to cut back our work week from sixty to forty hours. In other words, we have absorbed the employment-displacing effect of technology not only by shifting our demands, but *by substituting leisure for work.*

## Importance of the Tertiary Sector

The conclusion, then, is that the demand for labor reflects the interplay of technology (which exerts differing leverages on different industries and occupations at different times) and of the existing demand for goods and services. Typically, the entrance of technology into industry has a twofold effect. The first is to raise the *potential* output of the industry, with its present labor force. The second is to enable the costs of the industry to decline, or its quality to improve, so that actual demand for the product will increase. But normally, the rise in demand is not great enough to enable the existing labor force to be retained along with the new techniques. Instead, some labor is displaced and must now find its employment elsewhere.

There are exceptions, of course. A great new industry, such as the automobile industry in the 1920's, will keep on expanding its labor force despite improved technology, for in such cases demand *is* sufficiently strong to absorb the output of the new technology, even with a growing labor force. Then too, there is the exception of capital-saving technology, making it possible for an industry to turn out the same product with a cheaper capital equipment, thereby making it attractive to expand production and to hire more labor.

But taking all industries and all technological changes together, the net result is unambiguous. As Table 11-8 reveals, technology has steadily increased our ability to create goods, both on the farm and on the factory floor, more rapidly than we have wished to, or been able to, consume them, with the result that employment in these areas has lagged behind output.

Note how agricultural output has increased by a fourth in this period, in part because of the needs of a rapidly growing population, while agricultural employment has shrunk by almost a third; and notice that whereas manufacturing output has risen by over half, employment on the factory floor has slightly declined.

Table 11-8    INDICES OF OUTPUT AND EMPLOYMENT IN
AGRICULTURE AND MANUFACTURING: 1950 = 100

|  | 1950 | 1962 |
|---|---|---|
| Manufacturing output | 100 | 157 |
| Manufacturing employment (production workers only) | 100 | 99 |
| Agricultural output | 100 | 126 |
| Agricultural employment | 100 | 69 |

During this same period, however, our total labor force increased by over eight millions. Where did these millions find employment? As we would expect, largely in the service sector. Actual totals for employment in various parts of the economy appear in Table 11-9.

Table 11-9    NONAGRICULTURAL EMPLOYMENT: 1950 AND 1963
(In millions)

| Year | Secondary Sector (mining, construction, manufacturing, transportation, utilities, etc.) | Trade | Tertiary Sector | | Government |
|---|---|---|---|---|---|
| | | | Finance, etc. | Personal services | |
| 1950 | 22.4 | 9.4 | 1.9 | 5.4 | 6.0 |
| 1963 | 24.5 | 11.9 | 2.9 | 8.3 | 9.5 |

## Employment and GNP

We have seen how the long-run employment–population ratio reflects slow-moving changes in the supply and demand for labor, and we have had a glimpse of some of the problems these

forces may create. Yet all this has seemed somehow at a considerable remove from the problems of saving and investment and
credit creation that have absorbed us in the earlier chapters of
this book. How can we now connect the supply and demand for
labor with the fluctuations in expenditure and output that have
served as our focus of attention heretofore?

To answer the question requires that we shift our focus,
somewhat as in our previous chapter, on the determination of
GNP. So long as we inquire into the reasons why a society em-
ploys such-and-such a fraction of its total population on such-and-
such tasks, our inquiry must necessarily follow a historical course.
But once we take the general ratio of employment to population
and its occupational distribution as a given starting point, we can
ask the more analytical question: what increases employment?—or
the even more important question: what decreases it?

Let us then begin, as so often before, at the simplest possible
starting point, an imaginary economy uncluttered by many of the
complicating factors of real life, such as changing technology or
tastes. Then it is easy to trace the cause of changes in employment. They must be the result of changes in GNP—that is, of
changes in expenditure. In turn, we can trace these changes to
our familiar basic motive forces: fluctuations in investment spending or in government spending (or on rare occasions to spontaneous changes in consumer spending).

In point of fact, even with technology and all other complexities added back in, the volume of spending is *still* the single
most important determinant of employment. With the exception
of only the war years, with their special demands on manpower,
in every year from 1929 to the present, when GNP has risen, employment has also risen; and in every year that GNP has declined,
employment has followed suit.

But the impact of spending on *unemployment* is not quite
so simple as this over-all correlation of employment might suggest. We have already seen that short-run changes in GNP will
bring about short-run changes in the labor participation rate, so
that rising GNP can produce both more jobs *and* more unemploy-

ment. In the same way, a declining GNP will discourage participation and thereby "abolish" some unemployment by causing
people to withdraw from the job market. During the 1960's, as
we have seen, *unemployment and employment and GNP* all rose
from 1960 to 1961, and again from 1962 to 1963.

## Irregularities in the Population Age Distribution

Another reason why changes in spending may not be mir-
rored by changes in unemployment is that the age-groupings of
the population are not always the same. In some years there will
be relatively more job seekers than in other years, with the result
that a given increase in spending will leave more unemployed at
some times than at others.

This has particular relevance for the years now ahead of us.
If we compare the age distribution in 1960 with that for 1970 we
can see a very marked increase in the number of young job seekers
for whom additional spending will have to provide jobs.

Table 11-10    DISTRIBUTION OF THE LABOR FORCE BY AGE: 1960 AND 1975

| Age group | 1960 | 1975 | Per cent |
|-----------|------|------|----------|
|           | (millions) |  | Increase |
| 14 – 19   | 4.9  | 9.2  | 88 |
| 20 – 34   | 21.7 | 33.4 | 54 |
| 35 – 64   | 33.9 | 46.7 | 38 |
| over 65   | 3.1  | 3.7  | 19 |

Source: *Hearings*, Joint Economic Committee, 88th Congress, 1st Session I, p. 203.

Note that the ranks of *youthful* job seekers will be dispropor-
tionately enlarged during the years ahead. Young people will, for
a time, be coming onto the labor market faster than older workers
are leaving it, with the result that the proportion of the entire
population seeking work will temporarily rise. If the level of unemployment is also to be prevented from rising, there will have
to be an unusually large increase in total national expenditure.

## Technological Change

Our discussion of the supply side of employment allows us to understand why an increase in spending may not always be met by a proportional decrease in unemployment. But now we must consider an even more important reason on the demand side: technological change.

Why is technological change relevant to the demand for labor? One reason is that the introduction of new technology is usually achieved through the means of new capital investment. Hence, the steady process of investment, indispensable for the maintenance of an even flow of GNP, is a vehicle for the steady introduction of new technology into the economy. To be sure, not all investment incorporates technological change—some investment merely expands or duplicates existing facilities with very little, if any, changes in design or end use. Yet historically, investment and technology have gone hand in hand, the technology stimulating the new investment and the investment incorporating the new technology. In addition, much so-called replacement investment is actually the source of a steady upgrading of the quality of capital assets, as old and obsolete plants and parts are replaced by new and modern ones.

Thus technological change is closely allied with the ongoing flow of investment spending. But how does technological change affect the demand for labor? To answer the question it will help us to differentiate between two kinds: demand-creating technology and cost-reducing technology.

### Demand-Creating Technology

Let us suppose that an inventor patents a new product—let us say an electronic sensory stove that automatically cooks things to perfection. Will such an invention create employment?

We will suppose that our inventor assembles his original models himself and peddles them in local stores, and we will ignore the small increase in spending (and perhaps in employment) due to his orders for raw materials. Instead, let us fasten our attention on the consumer who first decides to buy the new product in a store, because it has stimulated his demand.

Will our consumer's purchase result in a *net* increase in consumer spending in the economy? If this is so—and if the new product is generally liked—it is easy to see how the new product could result in sizeable additional employment.

But will it be true? Our consumer has, to be sure, bought a new item. But unless his income has increased, there is no reason to believe that this is a *net* addition to his consumption expenditures. The chances are, rather, that this unforeseen expenditure will be balanced by lessened spending for some other item. Almost surely he will not buy a regular stove. (When consumers first began buying television sets, they stopped buying as many radios and going to the movies as often.) But even where there is no direct competition, where the product is quite "new," everything that we know about the stability of the propensity to consume schedule leads us to believe that *total* consumer spending will not rise.

Thus we reach the important conclusion that new products do not automatically create *additional* spending, even though they may mobilize consumer demand for themselves. Indeed, many new products emerge onto the market every year and merely shoulder old products off. Must we then conclude that demand-creating inventions do not affect employment?

## Employment and Investment

We are by no means ready to jump to that conclusion. Rather, what we have seen enables us to understand that if a new product is to create employment, it must give rise to new *investment* (and to the consumption it induces in turn). If our electronic stove is successful, it may induce our inventor to borrow money from a bank and to build a plant to mass-produce the item. If consumer demand for it continues to rise, a very large factory may have to be built to accommodate demand. As a result of the investment expenditures on the new plant, consumers' incomes *will* rise, and more employment will be created as they spend their incomes on various consumer items.*

When we think of a new product not in terms of a household gadget but in terms of the automobile, airplane, or perhaps the transistor, we can understand how large the employment-creating potential of certain kinds of inventions can be. Originally the automobile merely resulted in a diversion of consumer spending from buggies, the airplane merely cut into railroad income, the transistor into vacuum tubes. But each of these inventions became in time the source of enormous investment expenditures. The automobile not only gave us the huge auto plants in Detroit, but indirectly brought into being multibillion dollar investment in highways, gasoline refineries, service stations, and industries whose impact on employment has been gigantic (it has been estimated that one in every seven jobs in America is directly or indirectly indebted to the existence of the automobile). On a smaller, but still very large, scale, the airplane gave rise not alone to huge aircraft building plants, but to airfields, radio and beacon equipment industries, and others, etc., whose employment totals are substantial. In turn, the transistor gave rise to entirely new design possibilities for miniaturization and thus gave an impetus for expansion to many businesses.

### Industry-Building Inventions

What sorts of inventions have this industry-building capacity? We can perhaps generalize by describing them as inventions that are of sufficient importance to become "indispensable" to the consumer or the manufacturer, and of sufficient mechanical or physical variance from the existing technical environment to necessitate the creation of a large amount of supporting capital equipment to integrate them into economic life.

Demand-creating inventions, then, can indeed create employ-

---

* To be sure, investment will decline in those areas that are now selling less to consumers. At most, however, this decline can affect only their replacement expenditures, which probably averaged 5 to 10 per cent of the value of their capital equipment. Meanwhile, in the new industry, an entire capital structure must be built from scratch. We can expect the total amount of investment spending to increase substantially, with its usual repercussive effects.

ment. They do so indirectly, however—not by inducing new consumer spending but by generating new 'investment spending.*

Unfortunately, there is no guarantee that these highly employment-generative inventions will come along precisely when they are needed. There have been long periods when the economy has not been adequately stimulated by this type of invention and when employment has lagged as a result. We shall return to these dynamic inventions when we discuss growth in our last chapter. But first let us consider the effect on employment of another kind of invention.

### Cost-Reducing Inventions

By a cost-reducing invention, we generally mean an invention or an innovation that enables a manufacturer to turn out the *same* product with less factor input. The factor that is saved may be, and often is, land or capital. But the type of cost-cutting invention that interests us here is probably the most common and surely the most important. These are *labor-saving* inventions or innovations, changes in technique or technology that enable an entrepreneur to turn out the same output as before with less labor, or a larger output than before with the same amount of labor.

Do such inventions "permanently" displace labor? Let us trace an imaginary instance and find out.

We assume in this case that an inventor has perfected a technique that makes it possible for a local shoe factory to reduce its production force from ten men to eight men, while still turning out the same number of shoes. Forgetting for the moment about the possible stimulatory effects of buying a new labor-saving machine,** let us see what happens to purchasing power and em-

---

* We should mention one effect of demand-creating inventions on consumption. It is probable that without the steady emergence of new products, the long-run propensity to consume would decline instead of remaining constant, as we have seen in Chapter 5. In this way, demand-creating technology is directly responsible for the creation of employment by helping to keep consumer spending higher than it would be without a flow of new products.

** This is not an unfair assumption. The labor-saving technology might be no more than a more effective division of labor within the existing plant, and thus require no new equipment, or the new equipment might be bought with regular capital replacement funds.

ployment if the shoe manufacturer simply goes on selling the same number of shoes at the same prices as before, utilizing the new lower cost process to increase his profits.

If our manufacturer now spends his increased profits in increased consumption, we can see that there has been no change in total spending in the community. The consumption of the two technologically displaced workers has been replaced by the consumption of the entrepreneur, and the total expenditures of the community are unchanged.

Exactly the same conclusion follows if our entrepreneur uses his cost-cutting invention to lower the price of shoes, in the hope of snaring a larger market. Now it is *consumers* who are given an increase in purchasing power equivalent to the cut in prices. The lost purchasing power of the displaced workers in this case has been transferred to the community at large, rather than to the entrepreneur.

### Incomes vs. Employment

Thus we can see that the introduction of labor-saving machinery does not necessarily imperil incomes; it merely shifts purchasing power from previously employed workers into the hands of consumers or into profits. But note also that *the unchanged volume of incomes is now associated with a smaller volume of employment. Thus the fact that there is no purchasing power "lost" when a labor-saving machine is introduced does not mean that there is no employment lost.*

Is this the end to our analysis of labor-displacing technology? It can be. It is possible that the introduction of labor-saving machinery will have no effect other than that of the example above: transferring consumer spending from previously employed labor to consumers or to entrepreneurs. But it is also possible that an employment-generating secondary effect may result. Our entrepreneur may be so encouraged at the higher profits from his new process that he uses his profits to invest in additional plant and equipment and thereby sets in motion, via the multiplier, a rise in total expenditure sufficient to re-employ his displaced workers. Or in our second instance, consumers may evidence such a brisk demand for shoes at lower prices that, once again, our employer is encouraged to invest in additional plant and equipment, with the same salutary results as above.*

The moral is clear. Labor-displacing technology can offset the unemployment created by its immediate introduction only if it induces sufficient investment to increase the volume of total spending to a point where employment also rises.

## The Impact of Automation

It is in connection with our foregoing discussion that the much talked-of threat of *automation* becomes most meaningful. By automation, we mean technological inventions that perform increasingly complex and often self-regulatory tasks, some on the factory floor and, more significantly, some previously associated with white collar work. In the main, automation is clearly a cost-cutting and labor-saving kind of technology, although it has important applications for new products as well. But one aspect of automation requires our special attention. It is the fact that automation represents the belated entry of technology into an area of economic activity that until now has been largely spared the impact of technical change. This is the area of service and administrative tasks that we have previously marked as an important source of growing employment. Thus the threat inherent in the new sensory, almost humanoid, equipment is not only that it will accelerate the employment-displacing effects in the secondary (manufacturing) sector. More sobering is that it may put an end to the traditional employment-absorptive effects of the tertiary service and administrative sector.

What could be the implications of such a development? In simplest terms, it means that in the future, ever fewer people will be needed to produce the goods and services we need. The migration of labor from agriculture to, and through, manufacturing into the ever-expanding service sector would now slow down or

* Do not fall into the trap of thinking that the new higher demand for shoes will, by itself, suffice to eradicate unemployment. To be sure, shoe purchases may now increase to previous levels or even higher. But consumer spending on other items will suffer to the exact degree that spending on shoes gains.

come to a halt, since the service sector could increase its output without hiring a proportionate increase in workers.

This *could*, of course, mean massive unemployment. But it need not. Just as in the case of our imaginary society that limited its demand to agricultural goods and solved its labor problem by cutting the work week, so a society that no longer needed to add labor as fast as its demands rose could easily solve the unemployment problem by sharing the amount of labor it *did* require more or less equitably among its members. To be sure, this raises many problems, not least among them the wage adjustments that must accompany such a reapportionment of hours.* But it makes clear that, essentially, the challenge of automation is one of finding a new balance in our attitudes toward work and leisure, and an equitable means of sharing work (and income, the reward for work) in a society where technology is beginning to invade the last precincts of human skills. The solution will assuredly not be an easy one, although it is by no means inherently impossible.

## Unemployment in the U.S.

We have spoken of unemployment heretofore in a somewhat detached and analytic fashion. Now it is time to look at the actual figures in the United States and to consider how unemployment can be actively and effectively combatted.

Table 11-11 gives us the important statistics for our benchmark years.

The terrible percentages of the Great Depression need no comment here. Rather, let us pay heed to the persistent level of unemployment in the 1960's. As we can see, we have been chron-

---

* What society is trying to do in rolling back hours of work is to *share* work and incomes more equitably. This is good for those who would otherwise be unemployed, but it may not be so good for those who are lucky enough to have jobs at the time when unemployment becomes a problem. These workers will be glad to cut their work week, but not so glad to cut their pay or to deprive themselves of increased pay in order to share incomes with their new workmates. In actuality, this source of potential conflict is softened because the process of shortening hours stretches out over fairly long periods and is often accompanied by rising productivity. As a result, hours may fall and weekly pay remain steady. But of course, if hours had not fallen, employed workers would have enjoyed a rise in pay.

ically afflicted during the 1960's with much higher levels of unemployment than in 1929; and the trend, if we go back to the
1950's, has been irregularly upward.

Table 11-11    UNEMPLOYMENT IN THE UNITED STATES

| Year | Unemployed (thousands) | Per cent of civilian labor force |
|---|---|---|
| 1929 | 1,550 | 3.2 |
| 1933 | 12,830 | 24.9 |
| 1940 | 8,120 | 14.6 |
| 1944 | 670 | 1.2 |
| 1960 | 3,931 | 5.6 |
| 1961 | 4,806 | 6.7 |
| 1962 | 4,012 | 5.6 |
| 1963 | 4,166 | 5.7 |

What is the cause of this unemployment? There seems to be
more than one cause. In fact, all of the possible reasons for unemployment that we have studied in our text have a relevance to
the current situation. In part, our labor participation rate has
been high, especially among women, thereby swelling the job-
seeking labor force. In part, our total GNP has not been large
enough. In part, we have experienced a considerable amount of
labor-displacing investment. And other reasons that we have not
specifically studied may be added as well, primary among them a
tendency for wage rates to rise faster than productivity in some
industries.

## Combatting Unemployment

The uncomfortable level of unemployment in the U.S. and
the prospect of a rising tide of young job hunters during the next
decade have naturally turned attention toward combatting unemployment. Our previous analysis should enable us to understand many current proposals.

1. *Increasing demand.* We have learned that as a general
rule, anything that increases the total demand of society is apt to
increase employment. This is particularly true when unemploy-

ment tends to be widespread, both as regards geographic location and industrial distribution. Then the expansion of GNP, whether by the stimulation of private investment, or consumer spending, or government expenditure, or net exports, should prove the single most reliable means of creating more employment.

There is, however, a very important caveat to be added to this general rule. If the increased demand arises from higher investment in automation equipment, the rise in employment may be short-lived; for the new equipment, once installed, may displace more labor than was employed in the course of building it. Hence the general rule that demand creates employment must be cautiously applied when the demand is centered about labor-displacing technology.

2. *Wage policy*. Increased demand also may not result in substantially increased employment if the increased spending only creates higher incomes for already employed workers and not new incomes for unemployed workers. Even then, there will be some employment creation through the multiplier effects of higher consumer spending, but the number of additional jobs will be smaller than if the new spending originally were to make new jobs and not higher incomes for existing job holders.

But if raising wages can impede the process of job creation, can cutting wages encourage it? The question is not a simple one, for lower wages set into motion contrary economic stimuli. On the one hand, lower wages cut costs and thereby tempt employers to add to their labor force. On the other hand, lower wages after a time will result in less consumption spending, and will thus adversely affect business sales. The net effect of a wage cut thus becomes highly unpredictable. If businessmen feel the positive gains of a cut in costs before they feel the adverse effects of a cut in sales, employment may rise—and thereby obviate the fall in consumption spending. On the other hand, employers may *expect* that the wage cut will lead to lower sales, and their pessimistic expectations may lead them to refrain from adding to their labor forces, despite the fall in costs. In that case, of course, employment will fall. On balance, most economists today fear the adverse effects of wage-cutting more than they welcome the possible job-creating effects.

It seems, then, that maintaining wages in the face of an economic decline and restraining wage rises in the face of an economic advance is the best way of encouraging maximum employment. It is one thing, however, to spell out such a general guideline to action and another to achieve it. To maintain wages against an undertow of falling sales requires a strong union movement. But once times improve, this same union movement is hardly likely to exercise the self-restraint needed to forego wage raises so that additional spending can go into the pockets of the previously unemployed. This poses another dilemma for a market society in search of a rational high employment policy, and there is at this moment no solution in sight.

3. *Remedying structural unemployment.* Not all unemployment is due to insufficient demand. Some can be traced to "structural" causes—to a lack of "fit" between the existing labor force and the existing job opportunities. For instance, men may be unemployed because they do not know of job opportunities in another city, or because they do not have the requisite skills to get, or hold, jobs that are currently being offered. Indeed, it is perfectly possible to have structural unemployment side-by-side with a lack of manpower in certain fields.

A sharp debate has raged in the United States concerning the importance of structural reasons (as contrasted with a general deficiency of demand) in accounting for the present level of unemployment. Many observers have pointed out that the unemployed are typically grouped into certain disprivileged categories: race, age, lack of training, and unfortunate geographic location. The aged and the young, the Negro and the unskilled, the displaced West Virginian coal miner or Massachusetts textile worker are not quickly pulled into employment by a general expansion of demand. The broad stream of purchasing passes most of them by and does not reintegrate them into the mainstream of the economy. Hence the stress is increasingly placed on measures to assist labor mobility, so that the unemployed can move from distressed to expansive areas, and on the retraining of men for those jobs offered by a technologically fast-moving society.

Retraining is, unfortunately, much easier when it is applied to a relatively few persons than when it is proposed as a general public policy affecting large numbers of unemployed. Then the question arises: for what jobs shall the unemployed be trained? Unless we know the *shape* of future demand very clearly, the risk is that a retraining program will only prepare workers for jobs that may no longer exist when the workers are ready for them. And unless the *level* of future demand is high, even a foresighted program will not effectively solve the unemployment problem.

4. *Reducing the supply of labor.* Finally, the possibility exists of attacking unemployment not from the demand side, but from the supply side, by cutting the work week, lengthening vacations, and similar measures. Essentially the possibility held out by shortening the work week is that a more or less fixed quantity of work will then be shared among a larger number of workers. This is entirely feasible and possible, provided that *the decrease in hours is not offset by an increase in hourly pay rates.* In other words, once again a rational wage policy holds the key between success and failure. Shorter hours, coupled with higher hourly wage rates, will merely raise unit costs (unless productivity rises quickly enough to compensate). This will certainly not contribute to increased employment. Shorter hours *without* increased hourly rates, on the other hand, may make it necessary for the employer to hire additional help in order to continue his established level of output.

Shortening hours of work can be a policy of despair. If people do not wish to change their habits, neither in regard to the number of hours per week or the number of years in their lifetimes that they work, then the cure for unemployment is surely to expand the demand for labor and not to diminish its supply. If private demand is inadequate to this task—and in view of the flood of young job seekers coming onto the market, this is likely to be true for the years ahead—then public demand may serve the purpose instead. A large program of urban renewal, for instance, stretched out over twenty years and highly labor-using in its methods, could by itself and by virtue of the secondary demand it would create, easily offer employment to the labor force of the 1960's and 1970's—in addition to filling an important social need.

But an attack on unemployment that seeks to reduce the supply of labor rather than to expand the demand for it, need not be a program of retreat. It can also become part of a deliberate and popularly endorsed effort to reshape both the patterns and the duration of work as it now exists. Thus it may be possible to reduce the size of the labor force by measures such as subsidies that would induce younger people to remain longer in school or by raising Social Security to make it attractive for older people to retire earlier. Such policies can be useful not alone in bringing down the participation rate and thus reducing "unemployment," but in affecting changes in the quality of life that would find general public approval.

## The Long-run Prospect

Looking back over the past, we have seen a considerable stability in the fraction of the population employed in the United States. Closer inspection reveals, however, that this regularity veils many changes both in the demand for, and supply of, labor; and it shows us the very large decrease in the working time that our society has required to reconcile the need to, and the need for, labor.

Looking again to the future, we see the possibility of a technology that ever more artfully performs (and thereby renders redundant) not only the mechanical and repetitive activities of labor, but its calculating, adaptive skills. Thus it appears that we stand at the threshold of an age when technology will at last invade those areas of production that have heretofore escaped duplication, and that this challenge will coincide with a period when the supply of young people looking for work will reach unprecedented heights.

To cope with these strains will surely require not one, but many policies: the encouragement of private demand and, in all likelihood, the substantial enlargement of public employment; the articulation of, and pressure for, a moderate wage policy;

imaginative and well-financed programs of training and rehabilitation; and perhaps the adoption of measures aimed at reducing the participation rate of certain groups. Over the longer run, the maintenance of a balance between the supply of, and the demand for, labor is likely to require adjustments to a substantially smaller "normal" workday or workweek. It seems likely that these, and no doubt other, policies for coping with unemployment will constitute some of the main political and economic issues over the coming decades.

# 12

# *The Problem of Growth*

There remains for us to consider but one subject in our introduction to macroeconomics: the subject of growth. Actually, we have already been concerned for many pages with the main problem, if not the explicit theme, of growth. From the very beginning of our study, investment has been at the center of our focus. Up to this point, however, we have thought of investment mainly as the process by which savings were offset so that a given level of expenditure could be maintained, or in the preceding chapter, as the key to the dynamic process by which employment was sometimes created and sometimes destroyed. In all these considerations, *fluctuations* in the level of investment were all-important, a slowdown spelling recession and unemployment, an acceleration leading to the opposite.

Now we must see the process of investment in a somewhat different perspective. Whether it proceeds slowly or fast, investment consists in the addition of real wealth to the stock of wealth of the nation. Thus, so long as there is *any* net investment, our stock of capital is growing; and with a growth in our capital, there should come a growth in our capacity to produce. In this way we can see that the process of investment leads inevitably to a consideration of economic growth, and it is to this subject that we now turn.

## The Meaning of Growth

As before, we will want to familiarize ourselves at the outset with the general statistical contours of the issue. But before we can approach the statistics, we must first define *growth,* for there are, in fact, at least three different meanings that we can give the word.

1. *Increase in aggregate product valued at current prices.* This is the crudest measure of growth, for all that it indicates is that expenditure has increased over time. Whether that expenditure has been matched by increased real output cannot be ascertained until we "deflate" the dollar figures by an appropriate price index.

2. *Increase in aggregate product at constant prices.* This is the usual measure of national growth, and one that we shall use frequently in this chapter. We should note, however, that the process of deflating the prices of the products of one year to the "equivalent" level of another year becomes increasingly difficult as the length of time from the base year increases. Thus it is easy enough to correct the price changes in automobile output from 1960 to 1961, so that changes in the value of automobile production in the two years represent changes in output and not just in price. But it is another thing to do the same for cars in 1963 versus 1943 or 1923 or 1913. Over the years of a decade (and sometimes less), the qualities of goods change so markedly that it becomes increasingly meaningless to relate output in one year to output in another merely by adjusting for price differences. This cautions us against interpreting long-run series of growth as denoting more than a general indication of the direction and magnitude of changes in output.*

3. *Increase in per capita output at constant prices.* There is still a final refinement we may wish to inject into a study of growth. This is to divide the "real" increase in output by the

* Series for GNP in current and constant dollars are shown in Appendix II.

number of persons among whom it is shared. Only then can we begin to relate the over-all increase in production with a first approximation of the real benefits, the welfare it yielded to its ultimate consumers. Even here, however, it is well to bear in mind that the number of individuals that constituted the average household of the past was different from that today, so that *per capita* indices can also be misleading.

In addition, per capita (or even per household) GNP figures do not reveal the tax burden falling on the average family, and this too must be taken into account before we draw welfare conclusions from the data. Perhaps most important, the corrected dollar figures are far from representing unambiguous "utility" to the consumer. The value of war production, for instance, is included in GNP at its dollar cost, and therefore goes into the per capita figures, but how much "use" arms production yields to the individual is a nebulous concept. Equally misleading, the production of trivialities, of poptop beer cans and electric toothbrushes, are accorded an equal weight in our indices of output with the production of doctors' services or lowcost housing. Thus it is all too easy to conclude, from an uncritical acceptance of the figures, that a rising index of output denotes an equal rate of improvement in the quality and enjoyments of life.

We conclude, then, that the real growth of output—or rather, the *meaning* of that growth in terms of living standards— is not always easy to find. Nonetheless, the figures, when handled with understanding, can give use a reasonably clear picture of what has happened over the past. Let us see what the figures on p. 214 show, for the bench-mark years we have previously used.

### The Historical Record

The general line of advance is clear enough. We can see how GNP in current dollars has grown much faster than GNP in constant dollars, the difference representing mainly the price inflations of two World Wars. We can also see that with all price increases washed out, GNP in real terms has grown steadily and more swiftly than population. The per capita figures indicate that the "average" person is roughly twice as well off today as he was in 1929, but here we must be very wary. Households today have, for instance, fewer members than formerly, so that household incomes have not risen quite so fast as per capita income. More important, we must repeat that the quality of goods has changed so much—largely for the better—and the quality of life itself to such a degree—for better and worse—that precise intertemporal comparisons seem fruitless. Perhaps it is best to decline to make much of the arithmetical relation of one era to another, but instead, merely to draw the irrefutable conclusion that there has been a marked improvement in material standards.

Table 12-1     GROSS NATIONAL PRODUCT
(Selected years)

| Year | GNP current prices | GNP in constant (1954) prices | Per capita GNP (1954) prices |
|------|--------------------|-------------------------------|------------------------------|
|      | (billions of dollars) |                            |                              |
| 1929 | $104.4 | $181.8 | $1,493 |
| 1933 | 56.0   | 126.6  | 1,007 |
| 1940 | 100.6  | 205.8  | 1,558 |
| 1944 | 211.4  | 317.9  | 2,296 |
| 1960 | 502.6  | 439.9  | 2,436 |
| 1961 | 518.7  | 447.9  | 2,438 |
| 1962 | 556.2  | 476.4  | 2,554 |
| 1963 | 583.9  | 492.6  | 2,602 |

## Rates of Growth

It is interesting, however, to calculate the *rate of growth* of GNP over the past decades. The precise figure for the rate will vary, depending on the initial and terminal years (if we begin in 1929, for instance, and end in 1934, we grow at a negative rate); but over the long span, a fairly regular rate of average increase in output reveals itself. In Fig. 12-1, we see a profile of our GNP in constant (1954) dollars, from 1909 through 1961. The vertical axis, measuring GNP, is scaled in logarithms, so that a straight upward sloping line represents a constant percentage rate of growth.

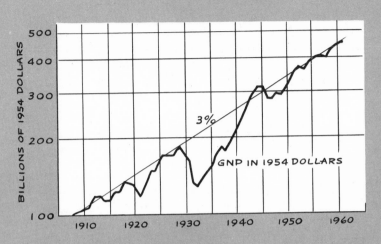

FIG. 12-1

As can be seen, a line that slopes at 3 per cent per year gives a very close fit, save for the trough of the Great Depression and the peak of World War II. If we take this as representing the average performance of the American economy, we can think of the effect of our average growth rate as doubling total output every 23 years. Total output *per capita* grows more slowly, of course, at about 1.6 per cent per year, doubling every 43 years on the average.

### Comparative Growth Rates

Is our rate of growth slowing down? Despite occasional alarm on this score, the statistical evidence does not show any significant decline in our long-term national growth rate.* Yet there is no doubt that our rate of growth over the past decade has not been good enough, as is all too tragically evidenced by the gradual rise

* In addition, let us stress again the huge changes in the quality of economic life. Think merely of the 50 per cent reduction of the workweek since 1900! Such far-reaching alterations make it difficult to speak with precise meaning about changes in the rate of growth of a decimal point or two.

of unemployment during these years. Moreover, a comparison with many other industrial countries shows that we have been one of the most sluggish economic performers in the 1950's:

Table 12-2    AVERAGE ANNUAL RATES OF GROWTH OF GNP

| Country | 1950–1955 | 1955–1960 | 1950–1960 |
|---|---|---|---|
| France | 4.5 | 4.2 | 4.3 |
| West Germany | 9.0 | 6.0 | 7.5 |
| Italy | 6.0 | 5.9 | 5.9 |
| United Kingdom | 2.6 | 2.7 | 2.6 |
| Japan | 7.1 | 9.4 | 8.8 |
| United States | 4.3 | 2.3 | 3.3 |

Source: from Stanley H. Cohn, in *Economic Growth: An American Problem*, ed. Peter M. Gutmann (Englewood Cliffs, N.J.: Prentice-Hall, Inc., 1964), p. 66.

Is there a reason for our relatively laggard performance? One reason may be that we are now "naturally" a country whose market demands turn away from those mass goods where productivity (and growth rates) are highest, and toward those kinds of output, mainly services, where rapid growth of output is less feasible with contemporary techniques. For there is no doubt that all the other nations on our list start considerably below us in terms of material levels of well-being, and therefore they may find themselves in the "high-growth" era of filling unsatisfied consumers' demands that have long since been satiated in the United States.

There are, in addition, a great many reasons of a direct and substantive kind that account for the faster rate of growth of many of these nations. Most of them suffered considerable war damage and thus had the advantage, by the time their plant was rebuilt in the early 1950's, of working with the latest and most productive capital equipment. As a result, less of their total investment stream was needed for replacement, and more could be devoted to still further additions to capital. Then, too, the burden of arms production was much smaller abroad than in our country. We must bear in mind as well that most European nations pursued growth-oriented policies more boldly than the United States. The deliberate promotion of growth was for most of them a direct political goal, to be achieved by fiscal or national planning measures of various sorts. Finally, it should be noted that the 1960's have seen an improvement in U.S. growth rates, although we are still one of the slowest growing of the industrial nations.

### *U.S. vs. U.S.S.R. Growth Rates*

One pair of growth rates has been the subject of much discussion in the post war years. This is the comparison of U.S. and U.S.S.R. growth performance. Estimates of gross national product for Russia are exceedingly difficult to make, since the Soviet Union does not calculate its gross national product as we do.* But regardless of considerable differences among experts as to the proper statistical interpretation of Russian figures, virtually all agree that Russian growth rates have been considerably faster than ours. Since U.S. output is probably at least twice as large as U.S.S.R. output, this may not seem to matter. But as the Figure 12-2 demonstrates, if a country with a small GNP has a higher

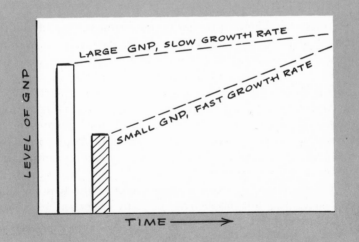

FIG. 12-2

---

* Following definitions established by Marx (who was himself following the line of thought of Adam Smith), the Soviets consider only the output of *goods* as "final product." Services, with the exception of the transportation of industrial items, are not counted. Consequently, much of the kind of output characteristic of a highly developed economy is not included in their calculations.

rate of growth than a country with a large one—and maintains it
—it is only a matter of time before the small country must
catch up.

How long would it take Russia to catch up with the United
States? That depends on what the two countries' rates of growth
will be. Table 12-3 makes a projection of various possibilities.

Table 12-3   COMPARATIVE GROWTH TABLE

| U.S.S.R. growth rate | U.S. growth rate | | |
|---|---|---|---|
| | 3.0% | 4.0% | 4.5% |
| | Year in which Russia's GNP will equal United States' GNP | | |
| 4.5% | 2013 | – | – |
| 5.0% | 2000 | 2039 | – |
| 6.0% | 1987 | 2000 | 2013 |

Source: Cohn, op. cit., p. 21.

What are likely to be the over-all growth rates of the two
contestants? Forecasts are not very reliable for either country.
Most projections for the U.S. use either a minimum growth rate
of 3 per cent, derived from historical experience, or a possible
growth rate of about 4.5 per cent, based on the productivity inherent in our new technology and on our expanding labor force
—assuming that we maintain full employment. Estimates for the
Soviet Union differ more widely, ranging from about 4.5 per cent
to 6 per cent, the latter figure being an approximate continuation
of Russian growth rates in the last decade, and the former figure
an estimate based on expected relaxations in the Russian effort
plus continuing low productivity in many important areas, especially agriculture.

Both the general estimates for the U.S. and for the U.S.S.R.
could be very wide of the mark, but it is important to note what
a difference a "few" percentage points make in the outcome. If
the U.S. achieves its indicated 4.5 per cent rate and the U.S.S.R.
slips to 4.5 per cent, the present relative level of the two nations

will be indefinitely maintained. But if the U.S. rate falls by only 1.5 percentage points and the Soviet gains 1.5 percentage points over its estimated low rate, Russian output will formally equate with American in only a little more than twenty years.

Is it undesirable for the Russians to catch up with the U.S.? So far as nuclear military capacities are concerned, the outcome of the race is apt to make little if any difference in the comparative strengths of the two nations. Much of Russia's gains from growth are likely to be reflected in civilian living standards that will still lag far behind those of the U.S., even when the value of Russian output as a whole equals that of America. Hence we can hope that a narrowing of the differentials between the two nations may lead to a lessening of tensions, whereas a maintenance or further widening of these differentials might exacerbate tensions. Prosperity may breed attitudes of political accommodation and social flexibility that failure will not. But these are questions for social psychologists and political scientists, not economists.

## The Causes of Growth: Extensive Investment

How does growth come about? We have seen how important rates of growth can be. Now we must leave our empirical inquiry aside and turn to an investigation of the factors that lie behind growth.

The simplest way that an economy can grow is to put more human and material resources to work or, more technically, to increase factor inputs. We are constantly doing this through the normal process of population growth.* Indeed, aggregate output *must* grow if the new members of a community are to get at least as large a share of output as the older members receive.

---

* In the short run, there is another way for nations to add to factor input. They can put to work the *unemployed* labor or capital they may have and perhaps achieve spectacular rates of economic advance for a while, until full employment or full utilization is reached. Between 1940 and 1941 in the U.S., for instance, GNP grew at the rate of 15 per cent. However, in considering growth as a basic economic problem, we are not concerned with such short-run spurts. Our interest is exclusively on the long-run possibilities for growth at full employment.

We cannot grow very successfully, however, if we try to use only the existing capital equipment for employing new members of the work force. To crowd a growing labor force into an unchanged physical plant or to combine the energies of a larger number of men with the same stock of machines would be bound to lead to trouble. Each increment to the working force would find itself less well-equipped than the previous. The so-called law of diminishing returns (or more technically, the law of diminishing marginal productivity) would set in with a vengeance, and the output of the new members of the work force would soon be far below that of the old.

To grow by adding labor input, as we do, each year, requires that we also add at least enough new capital to maintain the old labor-to-capital ratios. This kind of investment, intended merely to equip new workers with as much productive equipment as their predecessors, we call *extensive investment*. Its aim is to "widen" the amount of capital wealth, and its effect is to add to aggregate output by maintaining rather than by increasing per capita output.

## Productivity

Yet it is apparent that extensive investment is somewhat like running to stay in place. This is a great deal better than slipping behind; but if we want to *gain* output per capita, we must do better still: we must add not only more input but better input. The efficiency or *productivity* of our factors must be enhanced.

As we learned in the preceding chapter and as Table 12-4 reiterates, our inputs *have* been getting steadily more productive, both in industry and agriculture. On the average, during the

Table 12-4    INDICES OF REAL OUTPUT PER MAN-HOUR: 1947 = 100

|             | 1947 | 1962 (prelim.) |
|-------------|------|----------------|
| Agriculture | 100  | 235            |
| Industry    | 100  | 149            |

1950's and the early 1960's, our labor productivity (our rate of output per man-hour of input) increased by some 2.9 per cent a year, averaging industry, where it has been slower, and agriculture, where the rate has been very high. How important this increase in productivity has been in making possible our national growth is apparent in Table 12-5.

Table 12-5  SOURCES OF ECONOMIC GROWTH: 1947–1960

| Increase in: | Percentage change per year |
|---|---|
| Labor input in man-hours | .6 |
| Productivity, GNP per worker | 2.9 |
| Gross national product | 3.5 |

Source: Council of Economic Advisors, 1962 Annual Report.

The table shows that increases in productivity account for some four-fifths of our aggregate economic growth since World War II. The low labor input figure is, of course, partly the result of a rising rate of unemployment during these years, so that we were not putting to work as many of our increased numbers of workers as we might have. But even if 1947 rates of employment had been maintained, the role of productivity would still have been predominant.

*Causes of Improved Productivity*

What accounts for the increase in labor productivity? Generally, we can distinguish four principal sources.

1. *Increased skills and education.* In the short run, the dexterity, skills, and adaptability of the labor force make a tremendous difference in the amount of output obtainable from a given capital apparatus. Fiascos of production testify to the absence of these determining influences in underdeveloped areas where modern plants must often be opened without a trained work force. In the longer run, it is not so much skills as general education that determines the output per individual worker. Contemporary studies place more and more stress on the productivity gains to be had from education, and they attribute as much as one-fifth of the total U.S. growth rate to increases in the "stock" of education incorporated in the average worker.

2. *Economies of Large-Scale Production.* A second source of

increased productivity per unit of input is the magnifying effect of mass production on output. Typically, when the organization of production reaches a certain critical size, especially in manufacturing, so-called "economies of scale" become possible. Many of these are based on the possibility of dividing complex operations into a series of simpler ones, each performed at high speed by a worker aided by specially designed equipment. It is difficult to estimate the degree of growth attributable to these economies of size. Certainly during the era of railroad-building and of the introduction of mass production, they contributed heavily to growth rate. In a careful study of the sources of U.S. growth, Edward F. Denison estimates that today's economies of large-scale production add only about 10 per cent to our annual rate of productivity increase.*

3. *Deepening of capital.* We have talked of the "widening" of capital, as each new worker was given the necessary equipment to put him on a productive par with his fellows. Now we must add the concept of the "deepening" of capital, or increasing the amount of capital with which each worker is equipped. Clearly, if we give each worker more machinery and other types of capital goods to work with, we should expect him to be able to increase his output for each hour's work. Over the long trajectory of economic growth, increased productivity has required the slow accumulation of very large capital stocks per working individual. Thus investment that increases capital per worker is, and will probably continue to be, one of the most effective levers for steadily raising output per worker. But unlike the steady widening of capital, the deepening of capital is not a regular process. Between 1929 and 1947 there was no additional capital added per worker! This was, of course, a time of severe depression and thereafter of enforced wartime stringencies. Since 1947, the value of our stock of capital per worker has been growing at about 2.7 per cent a year.** As we shall see, immediately following, how-

* *The Sources of Economic Growth in the United States* (New York: Committee for Economic Development, 1962).
** Council of Economic Advisers, *Annual Report* (Washington, D.C.: Government Printing Office, 1962).

ever, the *size* of this additional stock of capital is of less crucial importance than the productivity of that capital—that is, its technological excellence.

4. *Technology.* We have just mentioned the fourth and last main source of increases in productivity—technology. During the past half century, GNP has consistently grown faster than can be accounted for by increases in the work force or the size of the capital stock. (Even during the 1929–1947 era, for instance, when capital stock per worker remained fixed, the output of GNP per worker grew by 1.5 per cent a year.) Part of this "unexplained" increase can be attributed to some of the sources of growth we have itemized above—mainly education and training, and economies of scale. But contemporary economic investigation increasingly attributes the bulk of the "bonus" rate of growth to the impact of new technology.

The term is, admittedly, somewhat vague. By "new technology" we mean new inventions of the demand-creating kind we have talked about, innovations of a labor-displacing (but productivity-enhancing) kind, the growth of knowledge in the form of research and development, changes in business organization or in techniques of management, and many other activities. What is increasingly apparent, however, is that the search for new products and processes is the main force behind much productivity-enhancing investment. Thus while investment has become less important for growth simply as a means of adding sheer quantities of capital to the labor force (although that is still a very important function, particularly in construction), it remains the strategic variable as the carrier of technological change.

## Changing Patterns of Growth

It is time to sum up what we have covered. We have seen that growth proceeds from two sources: *more* input and more *productive* input, and we have been concerned with studying some of the main facets of both kinds of growth. Perhaps we can summarize our findings in Table 12-6, comparing the sources of growth in two eras of our past.

Table 12-6     SOURCES OF U.S. ECONOMIC GROWTH

| Source | 1909–1929 | 1929–1957 |
|---|---|---|
| | *(percentage of total)* | |
| Total increase in real national income | 100 | 100 |
| Increase in labor force | 39 | 27 |
| Improved education and training | 13 | 27 |
| Increased stock of capital goods | 26 | 15 |
| Improved technology | 12 | 20 |
| Other, mainly economies of scale | 10 | 11 |

Source: Denison, *op. cit.*

Note the declining importance played by increases in numbers of workers or sheer dollar value of capital, and the increasing importance of the "intangibles" of education and technology. To a number of observers, this shift signifies that we have been slowly moving into a new phase of industrial organization in which productivity more and more reflects the application of scientific knowledge rather than the mere brute leverage of mechanical strength and power. Whether this new "postindustrial" society will continue to match the growth rates of the past or even to better them, or whether it will introduce a new era of slower growth is a question that we shall not be able to answer for many years.

## The Costs of Growth

But the question introduces us to a new thought. Heretofore we have talked of growth solely in terms of its benefits; and in a society whose total output is still not large enough to afford affluence to all, this is perfectly right. Yet before we move to other problems of growth, we should at least stop momentarily to recognize that growth is not costless and that the deliberate acceleration of growth may be a very painful process.

We can distinguish between two main costs of growth. One of these is the close association between growth and *change*. One of the clichés of American life is that change is an integral part of our system and that we welcome it as a sign of progress. This is perfectly true, so long as the change affects someone other than ourselves. But if it means moving from one town to another in order to hold a job, or learning a new skill, or taking up a new line of products in our business, then change is not so pleasant. All of these actions are attended with the much greater risk of failure that always goes with the unaccustomed. Yet such change is part and parcel of economic growth.

There is, however, a more profound and wrenching cost to be paid for economic growth. This is the cost of *sacrificing the present for the sake of the future.*

Investment, as we have seen, plays a crucial and indispensable role in the growth process. Yet, for all its usefulness, we must understand that investment, by its very nature, often entails a sacrifice. In a fully employed economy, the resources that we devote to capital investment cannot be used for current enjoyment. What is invested cannot be consumed. What is put aside to increase output in the future cannot be enjoyed today.

Note carefully that this applies only to a fully employed economy. *When there are unemployed resources available, investment will not be a sacrifice.* Then, men and equipment that would otherwise be idle can be used for capital-building purposes. Our commitment to the future can be made without any diminution of our enjoyment of the present—indeed, when there is unemployment, our investment will stimulate aggregate consumption output and thus increase the sum of present well-being.

Yet we can also see that once an economy has reached full employment, growth is no longer to be achieved costlessly. Now we can devote more men to the provision of capital goods only by taking them away from the provision of consumption goods. If our economy does this spontaneously, by raising its rate of voluntary saving, the problem is easily solved. By saving more, we simultaneously decide to consume less, thereby voluntarily relinquishing our demand for consumption goods at the same time that we facilitate the redeployment of resources into investment.

Not so if the community decides—let us say by voting for a public works program—to raise its rate of growth, but does not make an equally explicit and enforceable decision to raise its rate of saving. Now saving must be *imposed* on the community, so that workers can be moved from the consumption industries, where the spending of the public attracts them, into the investment industries, where the growth program needs them. Inflation, taxes, rationing, or some other form of control now take the place of saving as a much more unpleasant means of arranging for the inescapable cost of growth to be paid. Increasing our rate of growth above that which is consonant with our spontaneous rate of saving is thus far from a simple or an entirely agreeable process, once the wastes of unemployment have been absorbed.

## Maintaining Expenditure and Increasing Output

Again and again we have come to the act of investment as constituting the central process of a macroeconomic system. Now, at the very end of our inquiry, we must again study this all-important process, seeing it for the last time in a somewhat new light.

Previously we have largely considered the act of investment as a monetary flow, the purpose of which was to offset the gap made in the receipts of business firms by saving in other sectors. Now, in the context of growth, we must add to this picture a physical dimension. We must remember that as the monetary flow is being maintained, the actual stock of physical equipment is being increased, bringing with it changes in *productive capacity*.

That is, in an economy where investment yearly goes on at the same rate and just counterbalances saving, the level of expenditures (and income) will remain unchanged, but the level of potential physical output will be growing. And this poses problems. If total spending—and therefore total demand—is unchanged, why should entrepreneurs invest in new facilities? Would any businessman build a new plant if he thought his sales would not increase? That being the case, would not investment soon come to a halt, if the demand of the economy did not rise?

And to take exactly the same problem from the point of view of the consumer rather than of the businessman, how could an economy of *steady* incomes hope to buy back the *growing* real output that would be the natural consequence of continuous investment?

Here, then, we have something like a paradox. Unless demand rises, investment will fall. But in order for demand to rise, investment itself must increase—we are by now well aware that increases in income usually arise from increases in investment. Thus investment must rise to keep from falling! Or to put the same conclusion in a more straightforward way, an *economy that is to grow steadily must have a rising level of investment to keep its income and demand abreast of its growing capacity to produce.*

### Demand and Capacity

Is steady growth possible? Can an economy keep investing just enough more each year so that its demand stays even with its growing output?

In part, the question asks us whether a market economy will find the stimulus, the motivation, to go on expanding its level of investment, year by year. To this question of very great importance, we shall return. But there is another way of looking at the question of whether steady growth can be achieved. This is to ascertain the *rate that investment will have to rise each year in order to keep demand abreast of growing output.*

The latter question turns our interest to a tension arising out of two different changes in the economy, both stemming from the act of investment itself. One of these changes we are very familiar with. It concerns the multiplier relationship, the change in income and demand due to an increase in investment. This relationship determines how much investment must increase to produce a required increase in the level of income and demand. The crucial "variable" here, we remember from our analysis of the multiplier, is the marginal propensity to save.

### The Marginal Output–Capital Ratio

But the second relationship is a new one to us. It concerns the *increase in productive capacity that will result from a given expenditure on investment.* Unlike the multiplier, a relationship based on behavior (that is, on our marginal propensity to save or consume), this new relationship is primarily a physical or technical one.

Suppose, for instance, that the managers of a certain business decide to increase their plant capacity by $1 million worth of output, presumably because they expect sales to increase by that amount. The cost of the new plant and equipment they will need to produce an extra million dollars worth of goods has nothing to do with behavioral propensities. Rather, it will be determined by engineering, technology, organization, and such considerations. The ratio of the cost of the new capital to the required increase in output may differ greatly from one industry to another, or from one nation to another. In the United States as a whole, it is usually figured to be about 2 to 3, meaning that for the economy as a whole, it takes $2 to $3 of additional capital to get an additional $1 of annual output.

This relationship is called the *marginal capital–output ratio* —"marginal" because it relates to additions to capital and output, and not to the average ratio of existing capital to existing output. For our problem, however, it is more convenient to use the reciprocal of this relationship: *the increase in productive capacity that results from a unit of investment.* For the United States, using the figures just given, the ratio of increase in output to new investment is on the order of ⅓ to ½, meaning that for the economy as a whole, $1 of new investment permits an increase in annual output of from 33¢ to 50¢. In this form, the relationship is called the *marginal output–capital ratio,* the amount of new output that a unit of new capital is capable of producing.

Now we can see that the problem of steady growth requires the balancing out of two relationships. Investment raises productive capacity through the marginal output–capital ratio. Additional investment raises income and demand through the multiplier. Clearly these two relationships must be brought into balance. But precisely what balance? How do our two relationships influence the *rate* of growth required of the economy if it is to grow steadily?

## Balanced Growth

With the aid of some very simple algebra, we can work out the problem.

Let $\Delta O$ represent the increase in productive capacity that will result from the current rate of net investment. (We have already met the symbol $\Delta$ on p. 87. It means *a change in*. . . .) Let $I$ represent the current rate of net investment; and let $\sigma$ (read "sigma") represent the marginal capital–output ratio.

Then our first equation is $\Delta O = \sigma I$. This merely states that the increase in productive capacity ($\Delta O$) is equal to net investment ($I$) multiplied by the marginal output–capital ratio ($\sigma$).

Our second equation is more familiar. It describes the relationship between an increase in income and demand ($\Delta Y$) and an increase in investment ($\Delta I$). We remember that this relationship hinges on the marginal propensity to save and that the larger this propensity, the smaller will be its multiplier impact. We can now write this inverse relationship as follows:

$$\Delta Y = \frac{1}{s} \Delta I, \text{ where s is our marginal propensity to save}$$

(formerly abbreviated as mps)

We now have one formula relating the increase in productive capacity to the rate of investment, and another equation relating the increase in income and demand to the increase in investment. It remains only to relate these two equations to each other to find out what we want: the increase needed in demand ($\Delta Y$) to match the increase in capacity ($\Delta O$).

In other words we must have $\Delta O = \Delta Y$, or (looking back to our two equations),

$$\frac{1}{s} \Delta I = \sigma I$$

This last equation gives us the relationship that must hold if the growth of demand is exactly to balance the growth of productive capacity. If we now multiply both sides of the equation by s, and then divide by $I$, we get

$$\frac{\Delta I}{I} = \sigma s$$

This is the equation that expresses the rate of growth of investment needed to preserve a balance between the growth of demand and the growth of capacity.*

## Moving Equilibrium

What is the purpose of this algebraic exercise? We have been trying to discover if an economy that is steadily investing—that is, increasing its capacity to produce—can be in equilibrium. We learned that such an economy must also have a growing income to buy back its growing output. And in order to have a growing income, we know that it requires a growing level of investment.

Our formulas have succeeded in showing us the precise rate of increase of investment that will keep our economy in what is called *moving equilibrium*. If the rate of investment grows at a rate equal to $\sigma s$, we will be adding to demand at just the right rate to absorb the new output made possible by past investment.

In practical terms, what does this mean? If we take $\frac{1}{2}$ to $\frac{1}{3}$ as an approximate value for $\sigma$, and 10 per cent as a rough indication of the marginal propensity to save, then we get a value for $\sigma s$ of $\frac{1}{2}$ to $\frac{1}{3}$ times 10 per cent, or a rate of growth of $\frac{1}{20}$ to $\frac{1}{30}$, or as we usually express it, from 5 per cent to a little over 3 per cent. This means that demand must rise by this percentage each year to stay even with rising capacity.

Needless to say, these are not exact estimates, and the true equilibrium rate of the growth for the United States requires a painstaking determination of the marginal output–capital ratios and the marginal propensity to save. Nevertheless, our formula has interesting implications, for it clearly reveals that different nations (or the same nation at different periods) will have different equilibrium growth rates. If we take India, for example, where the savings ratio is much smaller than in the United States —perhaps as small as 5 per cent—we can see that an equilibrium growth rate (assuming that the marginal output–capital ratio is

* The idea was first formulated in 1939 by Sir Roy Harrod and then independently by Evsey Domar.

the same as the United States), will be much lower than in our country. On the other hand, if technology should lead to a rise in our own marginal output–capital ratio—that is, to an ability to win more output from a unit of investment than in the past—our rate of equilibrium growth will rise, for then we shall have to raise demand more rapidly to keep pace with a faster-rising output.

## Requirements for Steady Growth

Thus the idea of moving equilibrium gives us a more complicated picture of an economy in balance than the stationary conception with which we began. We can now see that not only must an economy generate sufficient investment to close the savings gap, but that the very act of investment creates the necessity for further growth. Moreover, we can see that growth can be too slow if income does not keep pace with output, with the result of falling prices and a probable slowdown in general activity. Or growth can be too fast, if incomes race out ahead of output, with rising prices and inflationary troubles.

Is it possible for an economy to sustain a rate of steady growth, avoiding both recession and inflation? It is apparent that the possibilities of straying to one side or the other of the line of moving equilibrium are great. Yet we can also see that shortfalls in the rate of growth or unduly rapid rates of growth can be corrected with the very same economic means that we discussed when talking of a simpler kind of disequilibrium. The use of the public sector or monetary policies to stimulate or retard the private sector will be just as useful in correcting a rate of growth as in offsetting a static imbalance between saving and investment.

We can also see that there are at least two other requirements for sustained growth. One of them is the obvious requirement of a *steadily growing supply of money*. If expenditures must grow to absorb increased output at unchanged prices, we will require a steadily rising supply of money to finance this expenditure. From our chapter on money, we know that such a rising supply of money can be made available by an expansion of reserves by the Federal Reserve authorities.

The other requirement for steady growth is concerned not with the mechanism but with the stimulus for growth. It is the need for *new technology to stimulate investment*. Without the stimulus of new products and processes, it is doubtful that investment would continue to play its dynamic role indefinitely. Rather, as the stock of capital grew larger in relation to the labor force, the productivity of the new capital equipment would decline, just as we would expect the marginal productivity of labor to decline if we kept adding labor to a fixed stock of equipment. In the face of a falling marginal product—and profit—for capital, the rate of investment would soon decline, and growth would falter.

All would still be well if, together with the decline in investment, came a matching decline in saving. Our rate of growth would still decrease, but there would be no fall in the absolute level of GNP. We would slowly reach a plateau of no—or very little—growth, with correspondingly little investment or net saving.

This is a destination envisaged for the economy by some of the great classical economists, such as Adam Smith and John Stuart Mill. But it seems an unlikely, if not unpleasant, terminus. As we have taken some pains to point out, investment is intimately associated with the act of invention itself, so that there seems little likelihood of a "piling-up" of capital to such a point that its marginal product and profit will seriously decline. Rather, the problem seems to be whether we will enjoy a stream of invention of sufficient importance to give rise to new investment in large enough quantity. For the foreseeable future at least, it will be the quantity of the new investment that will remain the critical factor.

## The Impetus of Growth

Will there be sufficient inventiveness to bring forth the investments required for sustained growth? This is a question we cannot answer. But it is well that we leave our survey of macroeconomics with the question itself well in the foreground of our thoughts. For as we look back on the long trajectory of growth of the market system, more and more do we locate the ultimate source of its energies in the creative, inventive quality of its technology and in the stimulus given to that technology by the institutions of a market society itself.

Is that trajectory now flattening out? Is the quality of technology today capable of maintaining a steady growth of GNP and an accompanying growth of employment? Will a more deliberate use of public powers have to supplement and maintain the strong, but unsteady, powers of the private investment? Will the market society turn toward the planning of growth over the years ahead?

These are the great economic questions of the future, questions that a knowledge of macroeconomics will not answer for us but will enable us to approach more intelligently. And perhaps at this last juncture, where our systematic instruction stops, it will be helpful if once again we ascend to that special vantage point of the economist and for the last time review the meaning of the economic panorama beneath us.

Again we see the interaction, on a national scale, of two worlds—a world of nature and a world of man—and we watch as man wrests from nature a steady flow of output, in part consumed by himself and in part added to his stock of national capital. We can now see more details than before in this process of interaction. We can see the role played by the techniques of output as they determine the manpower that must be allocated to different tasks and as they determine the size of the increased output that emerges from the widening and deepening capital stock. We can see as well the direct contribution made by man's energies and the slow change in the quantity and quality of that effort and in the groups of the population from whom it emerges. We can see the wants of man, not only impelling him to work, but in the guise of demand, acting as the guide for his productive efforts.

Then, too, we can discern the curious role played by money, the great intermediary in the process of production. And finally, we can make out the fundamental importance of men's habits and drives—their passive, predictable reactions to changes in their incomes; their active, unpredictable search for profits—as these, in turn, help shape the all-embracing interaction process.

Watching this process, we can see that the flow of output tends to mount from year to year, as each family consumes more goods and each worker labors with more capital. More interesting yet, this growth is accomplished in the face of a declining contribution of work-hours from each laborer.

What is it that regulates this critical alchemy between man and nature? Saving and investment—and behind them, the habits of households and expectations of businessmen; the demand for labor and the supply of labor—and behind them, the technology of output and the tastes and wants and needs of individuals; invention and intervention—and behind them the cultural fabric that has produced modern technology and that is now forming a new social technology of economic control—these are the fundamental forces behind income, employment, and growth. They are the forces that will shape the economic environment of our individual lives and of our collective destiny. If we are to control that destiny and thus to create for ourselves, as individuals and as a community, the kind of environment we want, we must understand the nature of these forces and how they act, one upon the other. That remains the grand objective of economics as an intellectual tool of mankind.

Gross National Product and Its Components*
(In billions of dollars; current prices)

| Year | GNP | Consumption | Gross private domestic investment | Government purchases | Net exports |
|------|------|-------------|-----------------------------------|----------------------|-------------|
| 1929 | 104.4 | 79.0 | 16.2 | 8.5 | .8 |
| 1930 | 91.1 | 71.0 | 10.3 | 9.2 | .7 |
| 1931 | 76.3 | 61.3 | 5.5 | 9.2 | .2 |
| 1932 | 58.5 | 49.3 | .9 | 8.1 | .2 |
| 1933 | 56.0 | 46.4 | 1.4 | 8.0 | .2 |
| 1934 | 65.0 | 51.9 | 2.9 | 9.8 | .4 |
| 1935 | 72.5 | 56.3 | 6.3 | 10.0 | — .1 |
| 1936 | 82.7 | 62.6 | 8.4 | 11.8 | — .1 |
| 1937 | 90.8 | 67.3 | 11.7 | 11.7 | .1 |
| 1938 | 85.2 | 64.4 | 6.7 | 12.8 | 1.1 |
| 1939 | 91.1 | 67.6 | 9.3 | 13.3 | .9 |
| 1940 | 100.6 | 71.9 | 13.2 | 14.1 | 1.5 |
| 1941 | 125.8 | 81.9 | 18.1 | 24.8 | 1.1 |
| 1942 | 159.1 | 89.7 | 9.9 | 59.7 | — .2 |
| 1943 | 192.5 | 100.5 | 5.6 | 88.6 | —2.2 |
| 1944 | 211.4 | 109.8 | 7.1 | 96.5 | —2.1 |
| 1945 | 213.6 | 121.7 | 10.4 | 82.9 | —1.4 |
| 1946 | 210.7 | 147.1 | 28.1 | 30.5 | 4.9 |
| 1947 | 234.3 | 165.4 | 31.5 | 28.4 | 9.0 |
| 1948 | 259.4 | 178.3 | 43.1 | 34.5 | 3.5 |
| 1949 | 258.1 | 181.2 | 33.0 | 40.2 | 3.8 |
| 1950 | 284.6 | 195.0 | 50.0 | 39.0 | .6 |
| 1951 | 329.0 | 209.8 | 56.3 | 60.5 | 2.4 |
| 1952 | 347.0 | 219.8 | 49.9 | 76.0 | 1.3 |
| 1953 | 365.4 | 232.6 | 50.3 | 82.8 | — .4 |
| 1954 | 363.1 | 238.0 | 48.9 | 75.3 | 1.0 |
| 1955 | 397.5 | 256.9 | 63.8 | 75.6 | 1.1 |
| 1956 | 419.2 | 269.9 | 67.4 | 79.0 | 2.9 |
| 1957 | 442.8 | 285.2 | 66.1 | 86.5 | 4.9 |
| 1958 | 444.5 | 293.2 | 56.6 | 93.5 | 1.2 |
| 1959 | 482.7 | 313.5 | 72.7 | 97.2 | — .8 |
| 1960 | 502.6 | 328.2 | 71.8 | 99.6 | 3.0 |
| 1961 | 518.7 | 337.3 | 68.8 | 108.0 | 4.6 |
| 1962 | 556.2 | 356.8 | 79.1 | 116.3 | 4.0 |
| 1963 | 583.9 | 375.0 | 82.0 | 122.6 | 4.4 |

Source: *Historical Statistics of the United States, 1929–1951; Economic Indicators, 1951–1963.*

* Alaska and Hawaii included after 1960. (Totals may not add, as a result of rounding.)

Gross National Product in Real Terms

| Year | GNP in 1954 prices (billions) | GNP per capita (1954 prices) |
|---|---|---|
| 1929 | 181.8 | 1493 |
| 1930 | 164.5 | 1336 |
| 1931 | 153.0 | 1230 |
| 1932 | 130.1 | 1042 |
| 1933 | 126.6 | 1007 |
| 1934 | 138.5 | 1096 |
| 1935 | 152.9 | 1200 |
| 1936 | 173.3 | 1352 |
| 1937 | 183.5 | 1422 |
| 1938 | 175.1 | 1347 |
| 1939 | 189.3 | 1445 |
| 1940 | 205.8 | 1558 |
| 1941 | 238.1 | 1783 |
| 1942 | 266.9 | 1980 |
| 1943 | 296.7 | 2169 |
| 1944 | 317.9 | 2296 |
| 1945 | 314.0 | 2244 |
| 1946 | 282.5 | 1997 |
| 1947 | 282.3 | 1959 |
| 1948 | 293.1 | 1999 |
| 1949 | 292.7 | 1961 |
| 1950 | 318.1 | 2096 |
| 1951 | 341.8 | 2216 |
| 1952 | 353.5 | 2254 |
| 1953 | 369.0 | 2313 |
| 1954 | 363.1 | 2236 |
| 1955 | 392.7 | 2376 |
| 1956 | 400.9 | 2382 |
| 1957 | 408.6 | 2385 |
| 1958 | 401.3 | 2304 |
| 1959 | 428.6 | 2421 |
| 1960 | 439.9 | 2436 |
| 1961 | 447.9 | 2438 |
| 1962 | 476.4 | 2554 |
| 1963 | 492.6 | 2602 |

Source: *Survey of Current Business*, July, 1964. Office of Business Economics, Department of Commerce.

# Index